Instant Business Letters

Second Edition

Instant Business Letters

Second Edition

Mary Bosticco

WILDWOOD HOUSE

First published in hardback 1968 by
Business Books Limited

Second edition published 1985 by
Gower Publishing Company Limited

This paperback edition published 1988 by
Wildwood House Limited
Gower House
Croft Road
Aldershot
Hampshire GU11 3HR
England

*The names used in the sample letters in Part Two are fictional. Any resemblance
to persons living or dead is accidental.*

British Library Cataloguing in Publication Data

Bosticco, Mary
    Instant business letters.—2nd ed.
    1. Commercial correspondence
    I. Title
    808′.066651021   HF5721

ISBN 0 7045 0602 5

Printed and bound in Great Britain by
Biddles Limited, Guildford and King's Lynn

Contents

Preface

We all know that cheese and good wine improve with age, but it is not often that a book gains in usefulness with the passing of time. Such, none the less, is the case with this book, for with the advent of the wordprocessor a great many of the letters in it can be keyboarded then stored in the machine's memory and recalled when needed time and time again.

This means that one of the aims of the first edition of this book, to cut down on dictation time, is spectacularly achieved in this second edition. The second aim was to improve on the quality of the letters you turn out and this aim still holds good.

The letters are all written out for you and grouped under the various subject headings. Within each heading, letters are separated into opening paragraphs, main paragraphs, and closing paragraphs. Each paragraph is clearly numbered.

Not all the letters are to be used in the same way.

- The sales letters in Chapter 3 should first of all be carefully read, together with the introductory section. Then the letters themselves should be mined for ideas, patterns, and examples to be used in compiling letters suited to your own product, service, and circumstances. This section can be referred to again and again as each new sales campaign is planned.
- The letters in Chapters 4, 5, 10 and much of Chapter 8 can be selected by you for keyboarding on your company wordprocessor and storage in the machine's memory for retrieval and use with little further intervention by you. Just jot down the numbers of the paragraphs you need and hand this book over to your wordprocessor operator. The book has been especially produced so that the pages lie flat, making it easy for the letters to be copied.
- Chapter 6, Credit and Collection, should be studied very carefully. Once you have done this, devise a policy and procedure based on it and suited to your own operation. You can then mark out the letters, or series of letters or cards, for typing and storing. Have them carefully marked 'Series One', 'Series Two', etc. and, within the series 'Reminder One, Two, Three' etc. All you will need to do then is to ask your secretary to

send out 'Reminder One, Two or Three' and your whole collection exercise can run smoothly with very little time involvement on your part.

● The remaining letters and the notices in Chapter 11, which are less routine, are not for storage and retrieval, but for individual use when the occasion arises. Simply select suitable paragraphs, jot down the numbers on your incoming letter and hand over both letter and this book to a typist. If your office is not equipped with a wordprocessor, use the book in this way throughout.

Details such as prices, brand names, delivery dates, etc. can be pencilled in by you next to the number of the corresponding paragraph. Your operator can then include these details in the finished letter by using the editing function in the wordprocessor or the typist can do likewise in the time-honoured way.

I have not felt it necessary to keep on repeating the 'Yours faithfully' or 'Yours sincerely' every time in the closing paragraphs; on the other hand you will find that some of the paragraphs under 'Body of the Letter' need nothing added to them to finish them off.

I should also like to point out that I have not always been able to avoid using a masculine pronoun, owing to the peculiarity of the English language. It goes without saying that where I say 'he', the same usually applies to a feminine subject. Absolutely no slight is intended to my female readers or to women in general. Being reasonable creatures they will undoubtedly realize this and possibly share my aversion to the constant repetition of 'his/her', which is distinctly ugly.

MARY BOSTICCO
Bourne End, March 1985

Acknowledgments

I should like to thank Atlas Business Machines, the British Railways Board, Nauticalia, Prontaprint, and Wordplex for permitting me to reproduce their letterheads or other material in this book. I am also most grateful for the help given to me by Fisher Clark, Ken Norman, John Rankin, and Carole Roffey.

Finally, no book could be written or revised without the generous help of the librarians of this world. Accordingly, I should like to thank all the staff at Maidenhead Library, and especially the Research Librarian, for their courteous and efficient assistance.

MB

Part One
The Business Letter

1

Appearance

Most business people like their company to be thought of as dynamic, up to date, and go-ahead, and, of course, a model of reliability and efficiency. Yet a great number of these same companies think nothing of sending out letters to customers and prospective customers badly typed on old-fashioned, poorly designed letterheadings.

The style is the company

Your letterhead represents the company. It speaks volumes and often creates the first impression which thousands of people have of your company – and, as you know, first impressions count.

What is a prospective customer to think if you write to him on a letterheading designed half a century ago, printed on cheap paper and with the letter itself badly typed and laid out to boot? Certainly not that you are go-ahead, up to date, and so on. How *could* you be?

Yet the difference in price between a shoddy, ill-conceived letterheading and one which is well-designed and professionally executed is not really so great. When you realize that a good letterhead alone can assure you of winning round one in any initial mail approach you make, then the cost involved will seem small to you indeed.

In a nutshell, your letterhead should indicate who you are, what you do, and where you are to be found, including by telephone and telex. More specifically, in the UK the Companies Act 1981 requires you to give the corporate name, if a company, the names of each partner, if a partnership, and your own name, if you are a sole trader. 'The Carparts Centre' or 'Florrie's Modes' on their own will not do.

There are other legal requirements: your letterhead should state where the company is registered, the registration number, and the registered address. Sole traders and partnerships must give an address where documents may be served. The VAT registration number, on the other hand, is only required on invoices.

In addition, your letterhead should convey the right impression of your concern; it should present the company image, if you prefer. You may feel that

Figure 1   The Nauticalia stationery

this word 'image' is becoming rather overworked and represents nothing but a gimmick, but such is not the case. You can call it what you like, but a company image is what customers or members of the public conjure up in their mind at the sight of that company's name. It is what people think of your company. Obviously it is up to you to make them think the right things, to conjure up the right image, in fact.

Obviously this image should be suited to your particular business. Some companies strive to create an impression, or an image, of solidity and reliability; a fashion house or a designer would be more interested in giving an impression of good taste, while a purveyor of luxury goods would want to exude an air of opulence and magnificence.

Ideally, your letterheading should not be designed in isolation, but should be part and parcel of your house style, whose task it is to present the right image of your company to the world. More and more companies are realizing this and many of them are acquiring a house style for the first time in their history.

An important part of the house style is the company symbol, or logo, which sometimes is a clue to what the company does, produces or represents. The Nauticalia House style is a case in point (see Figure 1). As you see, their logo is incorporated into letterheads, order acknowledgements, address labels and compliment slips. You will not be at all surprised to learn that Nauticalia Limited are manufacturers of marine artefacts. The name and logo not only tell us quite clearly what field the company is in, but the overall impression the house style gives is one of humour and cheerfulness, not a bad image at all for a company dealing largely with the yachting fraternity.

The company logo can and should also be used in advertisements and catalogues, on delivery vans, staff uniforms, and where pertinent, vehicles of all sorts. Airline companies and shipping lines use their logo on their planes and vessels and British Rail uses it on its trains. Figure 2 shows the well-known arrow-like logo on BR's clean, uncluttered, and up-to-date letterhead. If you use your house style in this way, gradually over the years, the general public is bound to grow aware of your company and what it does.

Colour is a very important factor in the house style and many companies use it on their letterheads as well. A house colour helps to make your company well known. Who, for instance, does not know that red is Woolworth's colour?

When having a letterhead designed, try to bear in mind that it never goes out on its own, but is always accompanied by a block of typing and a signature at the bottom. In other words, the text of the letter and the signature actually form part of the design and unquestionably help to create the total inpression. Notice in Figure 3 how beautifully the address block on the left balances with the one on the right, forming a harmonious whole.

In Figure 4 notice how the name ATLAS in the top left-hand corner is counterbalanced by the word U-BIX in the bottom right-hand corner of the letterhead. Both these words figure in bright blue on the original letterhead, while the WORDPLEX logo is in kelly green. The Wordplex executives sometimes sign their letters in green to match, while ATLAS people use a blue-ink pen, a small detail this, but telling.

Fisher Clark, the commercial stationery people, use colour with striking

British Railways Board Press Office
Rail House, Euston Square,
London NW1 2DZ
Telephone 01-262 3232 Ext. 7021/4

InterCity

C Bleasdale
Director

Figure 2   A British Railways Board Letterheading

Mr P C Thatch
Director Management Services
Kloot & Associates
Hollybush Lane
Basingstoke
Hampshire

13 December 1984

WORDPLEX

WORDPLEX LIMITED
Excel House
49 De Montfort Road
Reading
Berkshire RG1 8LP

Tel: (0734) 585242
Telex: 848560

Dear Mr Thatch,

May I thank you and your colleagues for sparing the time to attend the
presentation at Excel House last Friday.

I was most interested in your comments regarding your office automation
strategy, and trust that you found some of the subject matter covered of
interest and relevance to your plans.

May I take this opportunity of wishing you a very merry Christmas and a
happy and prosperous New Year.

Yours sincerely,

R.A. Winder
SALES & MARKETING DIRECTOR

RAW:LMK

A Subsidiary of:
Wordplex Information Systems PLC

Registered Office:
Marlow Place Station Road Marlow Bucks SL7 1NB
Registered in England No. 1773973

**Figure 3   A Wordplex letter, forming a harmonious whole with
the letterheading**

Atlas Business Machines Limited
Townfield House   Totteridge Road   High Wycombe   Bucks HP13 6EB
Telephone: General Enquiries (0494) 40116   Service (0494) 21871   FAX (0494) 24262

A subsidiary of the Atlas Business Group Ltd.

U-BiX
ACCREDITED DEALER
RELIABLE
COPIER AND FACSIMILE
SYSTEMS

A member of the Erskine House PLC Group of Companies
Registered in England, No. 1336132   VAT Registration No. 342 8374 49

Figure 4   Another well-balanced letterheading, this time from Atlas Business Machines

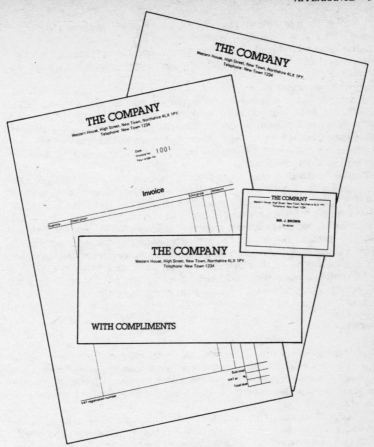

Figure 5   A Prontaprint business pack

originality. Their letterhead is embossed in brown on buff paper and letters are typed with a brown ribbon. The overall effect is so impressive that no one reading such a letter could easily forget it. Needless to say, the Fisher Clark logo, a sort of chevron, is featured also on every pack of the company's products.

Not all businesses have a symbol, of course, but all of them can select a modern typeface and an up-to-date layout for their letterhead. Designing a letterhead is not a do-it-yourself job, however. It is a very specialized and quite difficult art and you are no more justified in tackling it yourself than in attempting to extract your own tooth. Furthermore, an objective point of view is needed, since it is important that the letterhead should represent the company and not its chief executive.

A well-designed letterhead can be acquired quite painlessly and inexpensively nowadays, since even the smallest town has its own printshop. Most of them are part of a larger group with its own design unit. Prontaprint, for instance, with branches in over 270 towns all over the United Kingdom, offers three special business packs of stationery which would be ideal for even the smallest company starting up. The packs consist of letterheadings, compliment slips, invoice forms, continuation sheets, business envelopes, and business cards – all in a house style designed for you (see Figure 5).

Of course, if you prefer, you can have your house style designed by your advertising agent, who would no doubt be happy to oblige.

Paper

A good design can be ruined if reproduced on cheap paper. Conversely, a good quality paper can give an air of distinction even to a letterhead which is not die-stamped. It would certainly pay you, therefore, to select a good quality paper for your letterheadings. If you yourself are not a paper expert, let your printer or designer advise you.

If you send out hundreds of thousands of circular letters a year, then you will no doubt have to select something a little less expensive for your sales letters. This should not worry you unduly, however, since direct-mail experts have proved time and time again that cheaper letterheadings in no way impair the results of their campaigns.

Do not neglect colour, for it can be tremendously effective. You can add a touch of colour either by using it in the design of the letterhead, as previously mentioned, or by using coloured paper. In the USA the use of pastel-coloured cards for collection reminders is very popular. Coloured paper can be equally effective for sales letters and in the case of several letters, a different colour can be selected for each letter in the sequence, thus adding to their interest.

As for size, most companies nowadays use the international paper sizes laid down by the International Standards Organization. The most popular size for letterheads is the A4, which measures 210 mm by 297 mm. If necessary, you can add an A5 size for shorter letters. This is half the A4 size, i.e. 148mm by 210mm.

ISO sizes come in three series: A, B, and C. The A series is for stationery and printed leaflets, B is mainly for larger printed matter, such as posters, and C is for envelopes, to be used, of course, in conjunction with the A-sized letterheads.

All the sizes in the three series have the same shape, i.e. a rectangle with the same proportion between long and short sides. Each size is achieved by folding the next larger size in half. The A series is based on the A0 sheet, which measures 841 mm by 1189 mm or one square metre. The A0 sheet folded in half gives us the A1 size, the A1 folded in half gives us the A2 and so on. The resulting sizes are as follows:

A sizes	Size in mm
A0	841 x 1189
A1	594 x 841
A2	420 x 594
A3	297 x 420
A4	210 x 297
A5	148 x 210
A6	105 x 148
A7	74 x 105

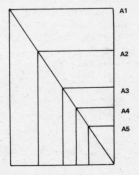

Figure 6   Diagram showing linear ratio of long and short sides of the "A" series paper sizes

Figure 6 shows how all the sizes in the A series have the same ratio between long and short sides. This means, of course, that the skilled job of scaling artwork to a particular sized paper is greatly simplified. Another simplification is the fact that as the master sheet measures exactly one square metre, it is possible to designate the weight of the paper as in grammes per square metre, rather than 1bs per ream of 500 sheets.

As far as the business world is concerned the advantages of the wholesale adoption of ISO sizes are the following:

1   Filing is greatly facilitated if all brochures, leaflets, and correspondence are in similar and related sizes.
2   Most European countries use ISO sizes and their filing systems are geared to it. This means that a British company sending quotations and literature in other sizes automatically becomes an oddity. If the British catalogue is too big or too awkward to fit in a prospective overseas customer's files, what will he do with it? Perhaps throw it out. So British companies cannot afford to be an oddity in export markets.
3   Scaling a piece of art work for use with various sizes of paper becomes easier and therefore quicker.
4   The Post Office's sorting task is speeded up, enabling electronic sorting equipment to be used at maximum efficiency.

Envelopes

Your business envelopes will, of course, match your letterheads in quality of paper, type face, and symbol. As we have seen, the C series of envelopes was devised by the ISO for use with the A series letterheads and literature. Unfortunately, while this mammoth standardization task was underway, the International Postal Union was quietly beavering away at its own standardization plan aimed at producing envelope sizes which would facilitate mail handling. Neither organization apparently thought of consulting the other, much less of working together.

The result is that in 1968 the General Post Office adopted a range of envelope sizes, known as Post Office Preferred, or POP, only one of which corresponds to the ISO C series! The POP range calls for an envelope which is rectangular in shape with the longer side at least 1.414 times the shorter side. A learned person from Christ Church, Oxford, once explained that this formula is based on Pythagoras's theorem and the fact that 1.414 is equal to the square root of 2. In order to verify that your envelope conforms to the POP specification, draw a square with sides equal to the envelope's length. The length of the diagonal of this square must not be less than twice the width of the envelope.

The Post Office recommends that everyone adopt the POP envelopes. It goes further and warns that any envelope outside the POP sizes will be charged extra postage. It must be admitted, however, that since this recommendation was made in 1968 the Post Office has not yet upped its charges to non-conformists.

POP sizes apply only to letters weighing up to 60 grammes. The minimum POP size is 90mm x 140mm and the maximum size is 120mm x 235mm. Envelopes should be made from paper weighing not more than 63 grammes per square metre.

Now that you are thoroughly confused and disgusted you should perhaps be reminded that there is on the market an envelope which suits the A4 letter to perfection: it is known as the DL. It is not an ISO size, but it does conform to Post Office preference. The DL size was thought up by the Germans many years ago and has survived all the major reforms in envelope size. Chaos really only breaks out when you try to match a larger mailing piece to a Manila envelope, as you will know if you have ever tried to do so.

If you do a great deal of business with European countries, you might consider using window envelopes. They are commonly used on the continent of Europe and have the advantage of saving a typist's time. They are not to be recommended for sales letters, however, since they have a dull air about them and do not encourage people to open them.

When you are sending out a mailing aimed at selling, the envelope should be made as enticing as possible. A real stamp is more interesting than a stamp mark from a franking machine. An unusual issue is more interesting than an ordinary stamp and a foreign stamp is more interesting than a British one. There is at least one world-famous company which purposely make some of their direct mail shots from Holland in order to give their letters that exciting foreign cachet. They should know, they have made millions through direct-mail selling.

One approach is to make the sales letter look as much like a personal or non-circular letter as possible. The foreign stamp gambit belongs in this category. Another, and equally effective idea, is to add an enticing message to the envelope, thereby giving away the game, but perhaps making the recipient eager to open the letter. One very famous international company has reply stamps peeping through the window of the envelope or uses an enticing illustration of a free gift with the words: 'Yours, absolutely free' printed nearby in red. Many companies use coloured envelopes and have such messages as 'Important news inside' or similar sentiments printed on the outside.

When dealing with direct-mail selling, the variations on the attention-getting theme are endless and it is a question of trial and error to establish which gimmicks work best for your particular product.

Reproduction

Time was when the only kind of letterhead a self-respecting company could consider was an engraved one. Those days are over, however, and you now have a choice of at least four methods of reproduction, all of them perfectly acceptable.

Engraving or die stamping. This is, of course, the Rolls Royce of printing processes. If you can afford the expense, there is nothing quite like it. It is the production of the initial master-die which makes engraving so expensive, but if you use great quantities of letterheadings the cost of having them engraved is not so exorbitant. If you needed only 1000 sheets, having them engraved would cost you about 200 per cent more than letterpress printing. If, however, you needed 10 000 sheets, engraving would cost you a mere 50 per cent more than letterpress. The cost of producing stationery varies from printer to printer,

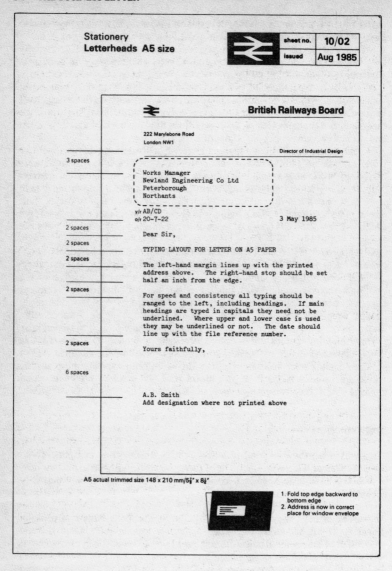

Figure 7   British Railways Board instructions to their typing staff

however, just like other services, and you would obviously want to get estimates from at least three printers before placing your order.

Thermography. This is the process called 'plateless engraving' in the United States because it has an embossed effect, yet is produced without expensive dies. This process is becoming very popular in Britain and it looks quite handsome. However, no knowledgeable person would mistake it for engraving. It is quite inexpensive, between 10 and 15 per cent more than ordinary letterpress, but here again, it depends on the printer.

Offset-lithography. Many companies produce their own letterheads and office forms on an offset duplicator. There is nothing messy, smelly or cumbersome about the modern offset machine. It is largely automatic and simple to operate. The result is undistinguishable from ordinary letterpress printing.

Letterpress printing. This is the conventional printing process we all know. You must feel perfectly free to use this process for your company's letterheads, since it is quite acceptable nowadays. A well-designed, up-to-date letterhead, printed letterpress on good quality paper, can represent your company very worthily indeed. In fact the letterpress printing process is the one most companies now use.

Typing and layout

The finest letterheading in the world, printed on the best quality paper, can be completely ruined by slapdash typing, erasures, smudges, and poor layout. Certainly, an ill-paid, incompetent typist is a poor economy indeed. But even a good typist has to be instructed on how your company likes its letters typed, both to conform with the design of the letterhead and for uniformity throughout the company.

First of all you will need to decide which is the best form of layout for your particular letterhead, and indeed you will have had the whole picture in mind when you had your letterhead designed. Now you will want the letters which go out to complement the design, forming a harmonious whole with it. Figure 3 clearly shows how successfully Wordplex achieved this aim.

Once you have decided on what the layout should be, you should instruct each typist accordingly. If you have several, it will pay you to have a letter of instructions typed for each size of letterheading used. Figure 7 shows how the British Railways Board does this, including instructions on how to fold the letter to fit the window envelope. The British Railways Board was one of the first British organizations to range its letters to the left. Now most British companies do so. This custom began out of pure expediency, but fortunately ways were found to render it not unpleasing to the eye.

Whether you decide on window envelopes or not, the address should be typed in block form, not in steps as was formerly the mode.

Your guiding principles in deciding on the layout of your letters should be to make them pleasant to look at and easy to read, while speed of execution should come a close second. It has to be admitted that a great many companies reverse this order of priorities.

Circular letters

A circular letter, if it aims at making a sale or bringing in inquiries, is just about the most important letter you can write. Yet because you may be sending it out in thousands instead of singly you may often feel you ought to economize as much as possible on its production.

Some economies you certainly can make, as previously mentioned. For instance, you can use a lower grade paper stock. If your usual letterhead is die-stamped, you can use the same design, letterpress printed, for your mailing shots. It might even be worthwhile having a special letterhead designed exclusively for sales letters, or you could try the very colourful special sales letterheads commercially available. Trial and error is your most valuable weapon here and if you are in the mail-order business it would certainly pay you to try various alternatives and keep track of results.

As for the envelope, there are two schools of thought, as we have already seen: you either aim at making it look like any other individually typed letter or else you permit it to announce itself as a circular and have some inducement printed on the envelope. The latter method is used with great success by many large and successful companies which sell goods and services by direct mail and is, in fact, in almost general use.

The one area in which you simply cannot afford economy is layout and general presentation. Moreover, you simply must make sure you have a full mailing list, including the name of the person you wish to reach. You can then address this person by name. With the facilities available nowadays there is absolutely no excuse for vaguely addressed sales letters with the address crudely typed in on top so that all the world can see it is a circular letter.

As for reproduction, the choice is multiple.

Wordprocessor. If you sell by direct mail or have frequent occasion to send out sales letters, you can do no better than to invest in a wordprocessor. There can be no question that this machine, with the appropriate printing unit and storage facility, will enable you to send out immaculate sales letters, addressed to the person you want to reach, all perfectly matched in and looking for all the world like an individually typed letter.

Your mailing lists can be stored in the machine's memory and retrieved when needed to be matched in perfectly with your latest sales letter.

The wordprocessor's editing function even allows you to add individual touches to the body of the letter, thereby making it even more personal to the addressee.

Do bear in mind, however, that there are well over a thousand different types and makes of wordprocessor on the market and they vary enormously. Before you buy one, therefore, it will pay you to make a thorough investigation of the market to ensure you are getting the facilities you need.

Stencil. Stencil reproduction has greatly improved over the past years and a well-typed stencil on good quality paper presents a very good appearance. It is now even possible to use a coloured ink on a stencil. Stencil duplication, for all its merits, is not really suitable for sales letters, but is perfectly adequate for reports, inter-company circulars and even internal newsletters.

Letterpress. This is ordinary printing, using a 'typewriter' face. The result looks like printing and no one could possibly mistake it for anything else. If you attempt to match in names and addresses, the result will be disastrous. With far more satisfactory methods available, there is no point in your plumping for this one.

Lithography. This process involves having the letter typed with a special ribbon. The resultant master can then be used to reproduce between 50 and 5000 copies. An older method involved typing the letter with an ordinary ribbon and having a photographic plate made from it. Whichever method is used, names and addresses can be matched in, with near perfect results.

Some litho machines can print the letterheading and the letter in the same operation, a very useful attribute when large mailings are involved.

Facsimile. This technique is based on letterpress printing, which we have already mentioned. There is one important difference, however. Once the text has been set up in typewriter characters, it is printed onto the stationery through a pure silk ribbon or sheet. The result is that the letters take on a slight irregularity of shape, as they normally do in typewriting. In other words, that absolute regularity which is characteristic of printing is eliminated and the result looks just like a typewritten letter.

There are two processes under this heading, the rotary and the flat-bed. Both give excellent results, the flat-bed process getting nearer to perfection.

Photocopying. The photocopying machine has wrought a minor revolution in offices all over the world, doing away with the tedious chore of copy-typing documents. To produce circular letters, you simply have the master-letter typed on plain paper, then feed it into the photocopying machine, stacking the letterheads in the feed-tray. Names and addresses can then be matched in.

If sufficient care is taken over inking the result is very good. Photocopying is by no means cheap, however, and is therefore best reserved for short runs.

The signature

The only other item you have to consider from the appearance point of view is your signature. If the number of letters going out is reasonably small, you will do well to sign each one individually. But this is out of the question where large mailings are concerned and the best solution in such cases is to have a facsimile signature in blue or blue-black. A typewritten name, a rubber stamp or a black signature produced at the same time as the body of the letter is simply not good enough and will instantly give the game away should any of your addressees have been labouring under the delusion that they had received an individually-typed letter from you.

Having given such careful thought to the appearance of your letter – the package, as it were – we are now ready to consider its content.

2

Content

Most business letters have a threefold aim:

1 To transmit a message from writer to recipient.
2 To move the recipient to action.
3 To imbue the recipient with friendly feelings towards the writer and his company.

A large percentage of the thousands of business letters which go out every day not only fail miserably to achieve aims two and three, but also seem to be doing their level best to defeat their primary aim – that of transmitting a clear and unequivocal message to their recipients.

Certainly, letter-writing is no easy task. If it were, fewer people would make such a poor job of it. Basically, your letters should aim for clarity, simplicity, brevity, and friendliness.

Clear writing is the result of clear thinking and, conversely, muddled writing is the result of muddled thinking. The first rule, therefore, is: think before you write. Decide what it is you want to say before you rush to put your thoughts into words or pen to paper. This may sound so very basic as to be almost an insult, yet innumerable executives complain that they have no time to think before they pour out their formless, inconclusive missives.

Try organizing the material in your mind before dictating it. Jot down the points on the letter you are answering. Mention one point at a time. Making three points at the same time is not brevity. It is muddle-headedness. Having made a point, move on to the next one. Do not paraphrase and regurgitate it at regular intervals throughout your letter.

When you have set out your arguments as lucidly and as briefly as possible, give your correspondent a clear and unmistakable indication of what you want him or her to do about it. Many a letter rambles on and on, stating and restating an argument and then just peters out, leaving its recipient wondering what is expected of him. If you are seeking advice on how to solve a problem, then clearly say so at the end of your letter. If you are simply setting out the facts which prompted you to act in a certain way, then make this clear also. 'I therefore decided to do thus and so,' you can conclude, thereby making it perfectly clear to your correspondent that all he is being asked to do is to take due note and need do nothing more. Obviously, if the situation warrants it, you will add '. . . and I hope you will approve of my decision'.

If you want to influence your correspondent's decision you must not fail to say so quite definitely: 'I therefore recommend that we do thus and so.' Or you can make it even stronger: 'I therefore feel that it is most important that we do this and that.' If all you want is a reply to your letter, then make that clear, too. Don't leave your correspondent with an unanswered 'So what?' on his lips when he has read your letter.

Your choice of words

The lucidity and conciseness of your letters will obvio: sly depend a great deal on your choice of words, but first of all you would do well to make a habit of using as few words as are necessary to express your meaning. Every word should earn its keep and there is no room in a crisp piece of writing for parasite words which do not add anything to your meaning.

Superfluous words are hard to get rid of. They only go by determined effort on your part. Read over every sentence of your letter and ask yourself: 'Is this word really necessary? Will the meaning change if I throw it out?' If your answer is 'No', then ruthlessly remove the redundant word. Your writing will gain a great deal in crispness and lucidity by this pruning operation.

If you were to take this advice to heart and begin re-reading your letters with a blue pencil in hand, your pruning operation would no doubt result in the demise of a good many worn-out clichés, those hardy fossils of 'commercial English' which still haunt far too many business letters. Clichés are the lazy person's tool. They spring all too readily to mind, rescuing the writer from the effort of thinking for himself. Throw them out before they cast their leaden imprint on your prose. Here is a short collection of undesirable clichés:

and oblige (as a close)
as and from
as per
as stated above
assuring you of our best
   attention
at an early date
at hand
at the present time
at this writing
at your earliest convenience
attached please find
avail yourself of this opportunity
await the pleasure of a reply
awaiting the favour of your further
   esteemed commands

beg to acknowledge

beg to advise
beg to announce
beg to remain (before
   complimentary close)

carefully noted
communication (instead of letter)
complying with your request
contents duly noted

deem it advisable
desire to state
due to the fact that

enclosed herewith
enclosed please find
esteemed favour
even date

favour (instead of letter)

has come to hand
has gone forward
has greatly helped
have before me
having regard to the fact
herewith enclose
herewith please find
hoping to be favoured

if and when
in answer to same
in connection therewith
in due course
in receipt of
in reply to yours
in reply I wish to state
in the near future
in the not too distant future
in this connection
instant (meaning this month)

kind favour
kindly advise
kindly be advised
kindly inform

meet your approval

note with interest
note with pleasure

of even date
our records show
owing to the fact that

past favours
permit me to state
please advise
please be advised
please find enclosed
please rest assured
proximo (for next month)
pursuant to

recent date
referring to your favour

referring to yours
regarding your communication
regret to advise
regret to state
replying to your favour
replying to yours

said (e.g. said package)
same (used as a pronoun)
submit herewith

take pleasure in advising
take this opportunity
thank you kindly
the writer
this is to advise you
to hand
trusting this will

ultimo
under separate cover
upon receipt of

valued favour
valued patronage

we note
we take pleasure
well and truly
when and as
wherein we state
wish to acknowledge
wish to advise
wish to state
would advise
would state
would suggest

your esteemed communication
your esteemed favour
your favour to hand
your goodself
your letter of even date
your valued inquiry
yours just to hand
yours of the fourth
yours to hand

For the benefit of readers whose mother tongue is not English, this is what to do about some of the most common of the preceding clichés:

at an early date	soon, shortly, or better still, be specific and say when
at hand	has arrived
at the present time	now or at the moment
at your earliest convenience	as soon as possible or leave out altogether if you are not in a hurry
beg	Do not beg at all, simply go ahead, and say your piece.
communication	letter or postcard, as the case may be
desire to state	This comes under the same heading as 'begging'. Do not desire to state, but go right ahead and state.
has come to hand	has arrived or has reached us
has gone forward	has been shipped, mailed, dispatched, as the case may be; otherwise, has been sent or other straightforward expression
herewith please find	we are enclosing, or other direct expression
in the near future	soon, shortly, or be more specific
note with interest	we were interested to learn
note with pleasure	we were pleased to learn, or hear
permit me to state, and the *'please be advised'* group	All of these come under the same heading as 'begging'. Just cut out the deadwood and boldly make your statement.
regret to advise	we are sorry to have to tell you, or words to that effect
regret to state	ditto
take pleasure in advising	we are pleased to inform you, let you know or even advise you, if you wish
the writer (meaning the writer of this letter)	just plain 'I'
under separate cover	separately or specify what kind of a 'cover' you mean, i.e. in a separate package, by parcel post and so on
wish to acknowledge and the rest of this group	This group also comes under the same heading as 'begging'. Just cut out the surplus words.
your goodself or *goodselves*	you

Most of the other phrases simply need taking out bodily like the deadwood they are. This does not mean, however, that every single cliché in the English language should be shunned by the careful writer. As Eric Partridge* points out, what is a cliché is partly a matter of opinion. If you have given careful

---

Dictionary of Clichés, Routledge and Kegan Paul, 5th edition, 1978.

thought to what you want to say and a well-used phrase conveys your meaning to perfection, then no one can fault you for using it. If, on the other hand, you use a cliché because it is the first thing that comes to mind, then your writing is in danger of becoming woolly.

Cultivate the habit of looking up the word you want to use in the dictionary. You will be surprised to find how often it does not convey the exact shade of meaning you have in mind. Decide whether you really mean *integrate* or whether *join, combine, amalgamate* do not convey your meaning more exactly. Don't plump for *alternative* without first considering *other, new, fresh, revised, different.*

Bear in mind that *verbal* means 'in words', as in: 'He did not give a verbal assent, but merely nodded.' It is often wrongly used for *oral,* i.e. spoken as distinct from written.

In choosing an adjective, try to find one that conveys the exact shade of meaning you want. *Nice* means absolutely nothing, of course, since we talk of a 'nice steak', a 'nice girl', a 'nice garden', and even a 'nice order'. *Overall* can mean either nothing at all or one of several things. If you really mean *total, average,* or *aggregate,* then why not say so? If you feel tempted to write: 'The overall growth of the city should be restrained' – don't. If you go over this sentence with your blue pencil as suggested you will find that the word *overall* contributes not one iota to the meaning.

If two words convey your meaning equally well, choose the shorter of the two. Short words are frequently more forceful and direct than longer ones because they have been part of the English language longer. They also contribute to better understanding of the written word, as Rudolph Flesch* has pointed out.

Sir Winston Churchill was a great advocate of the short word, although he certainly did not disdain to use a long one, even a very long one, if it suited his purpose.

Think twice, therefore, before peppering your letters with long words with prefixes and suffixes of non-English origin, such as *pre, re, de,* or *ousness* and *ization.* Do not be afraid of using the words *say* and *tell* in preference to *state, inform* or *acquaint.* Do not hesitate to use *begin* or *start* in place of *commence.* Certainly say *outline* or *sketch* rather than *adumbrate*; *plan* rather than *blueprint*; *before* rather than *prior to*; *about* rather than *regarding, respecting* or *concerning.*

Remember the trick of adding an adverb to a verb in order to create a totally different verb. You can then write *get up, get down, get better* instead of using the longer, Latin-derived equivalents.

If you ever feel you are losing face by using a short simple word, remember Sir Ernest Gowers' acid comment: 'Those who run to long words are mainly the unskilled and tasteless. They confuse pomposity with dignity, flaccidity with ease, and bulk with force.'

In choosing your words, then, prefer the short word to the long, the simple to the complex, the familiar to the uncommon.

The Art of Readable Writing, Harper and Row, Silver Jubilee Edition, 1974. *The Art of Plain Talk*, Harper and Row, 1962.

Other considerations

Together with the short word, favour the short sentence. It is more up to date than longer ones, since the English sentence has been getting shorter and shorter over the past centuries. But there is another reason to favour the shorter sentence. It has been conclusively proved that a piece of writing containing mainly short sentences is easier to understand, i.e. more readable, than one containing longer ones.

Several studies have been made over the years on what makes a piece of writing easy to read. The famous Flesch Readability Formula takes into consideration not only sentence length, but also the number of words with affixes. The shorter the sentences and the fewer words with affixes, the easier a piece of writing is to read.

Robert Gunning made a similar study, which he called the Fog Index. It is based entirely on the length of the sentences in a given passage and the conclusions reached are identical with those of Flesch.

So make your sentences as short as possible to begin with. Gradually, over the months and the years, you will find them lengthening without loss of clarity. Your ultimate aim will be to alternate between sentences of different lengths for greater variety and flexibility.

Certainly if you bear in mind all the above points, your letters should gradually gain in clarity, brevity and simplicity. But this threefold aim is unfortunately not enough. You will also want to sound warm and friendly, rather than distant and impersonal. There is a trend in some quarters to write curt letters. Do not follow it.

It frequently happens that you meet a business person whom you find to be charming, friendly and warm. You discuss a business matter, reach agreement and then go your respective ways. The following morning you receive a cold, stiff letter confirming the agreement made. It is signed by the same warm, charming person you met the day before, but it doesn't sound like it at all.

Why do some people write in this way? Why do they not put their warm and pleasant manner across in their letters? Because they are hiding behind the cold facade of what they think is 'commercial English'. If they were to use a pleasant conversational tone and write as they speak, their personality would automatically come across and you would read their letters with a great deal more pleasure.

Try it yourself and see. No less an authority than Sir Winston Churchill advocated the practice. This is what he once advised during his premiership: 'Let us not shrink from using the short expressive phrase even if it is conversational.'

This does not mean, of course, that you should write to everyone in the same way, or that a professional person should suddenly start dashing off little notes in a gay abondoned style. It means, rather, that you should be aware of your audience every time you write a letter – and do bear in mind that not every executive is a man. The professional writer always 'angles' his writing to suit his audience. In other words, he does not write in a vacuum, but to a specific public. The business person should do the same when answering correspondence. He should aim to make every letter he writes a sales letter – a letter which sells his company, his products, and himself.

Above all, always remember to write your letters from the point of view of your correspondent. Say: 'You will be pleased to know that your order is now ready for shipment', rather than 'I am pleased to inform you . . .' Most business letters are peppered throughout with 'I's and 'we's, as if the writer had no other thought but himself. Yet your correspondent is interested in *himself*, he wants to know what there is in it for him.

On the other hand, by all means prefer an I or a we as the subject of your verbs and only use the passive voice when you cannot avoid it. The active voice is so much more forceful and direct. It is always a person or a group who does, feels, decides, thinks and so on. Make this person or group the subject of your sentence whenever possible.

As for the actual rules of grammar, it is as well not to be too sensitive about them, since uncertainty about the correct usage will often result in woolly and verbose letters. While a basic knowledge of grammar is obviously useful, it is also comforting to bear in mind that the world will not cave in if you ignore one of the rules. Some of the greatest writers in the English language, from Shakespeare down, have from time to time ignored the rules of grammar. It is far more important that you 'come through' to your correspondent as you really are, as the person he or she knows. If you happen to be a rough diamond, your correspondent will be disconcerted if you write letters like a college professor. If you are cheerful and informal your correspondent will be chilled if you write one of those old-fashioned, jargon-infested missives. In brief, the golden rule 'be yourself' should also apply to letter writing.

Capitals

The trend is to cut down on capital letters. Use an initial capital for:

1 Proper names of persons, countries, towns, cities, villages, counties, rivers, mountains, lakes, seas, and oceans.
2 The names of months and days of the week.
3 The titles of books, plays, articles, magazines, chapters in books, speeches, operas, songs, etc. e.g. 'His favourite play is *Othello*.' 'The best book on the subject is *Investing Made Easy*.'
4 The names of ships, houses, hotels, restaurants, inns, etc.
5 A common noun when it is used in conjunction with a proper name, e.g. Oxford Street, Mount Everest, Waterloo Station. Or when it is used in place of a proper name, e.g. 'The Company has six directors' – meaning Company X.
6 A designation of rank or position when it is used in conjunction with a proper name, e.g. 'Major Harris has just been appointed to the Board of Directors.' Or when it refers to a specific person, e.g. 'The Queen's trip to the West Indies.'

Do *not* use capitals for:

1 A common noun when it is used to indicate a general category of persons or things, e.g. 'There are many universities in Great Britain.'
2 A designation of rank or position when it is used as a common noun, e.g. 'Some managing directors have worked their way up from the bottom.'
3 The names of the various disciplines when used in a general sense, e.g. 'He is reading history and economics.'

In case of doubt, the only course to follow is to use your own discretion, bearing in mind the trend towards fewer capitals. Once your decision is made, stick to it throughout your letter. An excellent practice, both with regard to spellings and capitals, is to follow one expert all the time and to advise your staff to do likewise. A great many authors and editors, for instance, are guided by the *Oxford Dictionary for Writers and Editors* (Oxford University Press) which is based on the *Oxford English Dictionary*. It is a small book, costing very little, and it would not therefore represent any great investment to have one in every department concerned with correspondence. It is familiarly known as 'Collins' to its faithful users, the original editions having been compiled by F. Howard Collins.

Punctuation

A whole book could be written on punctuation alone. In fact, such a book has been written. It is *Mind the Stop** by G. V. Carey, also available in paperback form. But the business person, who is mainly concerned with writing business letters and memoranda, does not need to make a deep study of punctuation. A few commonsense pointers are all that is needed.

Full stop. The trend is towards making less use of punctuation marks. The only exception is the full stop, which is getting more exercise because of the shorter sentences now in vogue. The full stop is also used after initials and most abbreviations. If an abbreviation ends as a word normally would, then no full stop is necessary. Hence: Nov., Mon., a.m., but Mr, Dr, Mme (no point). However, in the interests of speed, these stops too are being left out more and more in business correspondence. We therefore now get RIBA, EEC, BA, and so on. The *Oxford Dictionary for Writers and Editors* is an excellent guide on this subject.

Comma. This punctuation mark indicates the shortest pause of all and was once used very extensively. Now, partly because of the advent of the shorter sentence and partly, perhaps, because in this age it seems a crime to wish to pause for anything, however briefly, the comma is much less used. It is quite wrong, however, to banish it entirely, since clarity sometimes calls for it. As a

---

* Cambridge University Press, 1958, Penguin Reference Books, 1976.

rule of thumb you might say that if the omission of a comma alters the meaning, then put it in. You need a comma to separate a list of items, e.g. 'Our factory manufactures nuts, bolts, hinges, nails, and screws'. Most authorities agree that you need a comma before the 'and' in the example given, although there are some die-hards who insist that it is not necessary. When only two items are listed, a comma is not needed, e.g. 'Eggs and ham', 'Tea and toast'.

Many good writers do not enclose short explanatory phrases between commas and if your meaning is perfectly clear you can safely leave the commas out. However, you must do one thing or the other, not put a comma before the phrase and leave it out at the end. Many people do this and it is an untidy habit. Write either: 'Mr James Whitman, our new export manager, will be visiting you early next month.' Or: 'Mr James Whitman our new export manager will be visiting you early next month.' This sentence clearly benefits from the insertion of a comma after 'Whitman' and 'manager'. The following sentence needs the two commas even more: 'Mr Smedley, whom I believe you met at our press party, will also be with us at the meeting.'

A comma also belongs before a direct quotation, e.g. 'He said, "See you tomorrow".' Remarks separating two halves of a direct quotation also call for a comma, e.g.'See you at the conference,' he said, 'and don't be late.' When addressing someone, the name or title of the person addressed needs a comma both before and after it, e.g. 'You will agree, gentlemen, that this has been a very difficult year.'

Semicolon. This punctuation mark indicates a pause somewhat shorter than a full stop, yet longer than a comma. The modern trend to short sentences has all but retired it, especially in business letters. If you find that your sentence is so long that you have to break it up with semicolons, you would do better to recast it into several short sentences.

There are occasions, however, even in the business letter, when a semicolon contributes to clarity and in such cases you should not hesitate to use it. If, for instance, you are listing several items, each of which you want to describe briefly, your sentence will be clearer if you divide each item with a semicolon and the material pertaining to each item with commas. You could, for instance, write: 'Our sales force is quite a small one: Smith, Jones, and Brown, who take care of the South; King, Bishop, and Lane, who cover the Midlands and the North; and McGregor, who takes care of Scotland single-handed.'

Sometimes the semicolon very definitely indicates a longer pause. This happens when you leave out a word. If you say:'We have six representatives to cover England and Wales, but only one to cover the whole of Scotland', a comma will do admirably. If you omit the 'but', however, a longer pause will be needed and consequently a semicolon will serve your purpose better, e.g. 'We have six representatives to cover England and Wales; only one to cover the whole of Scotland.'

Colon. The colon indicates a pause somewhat longer than a semicolon but not quite so long as a full stop. You will seldom need to use it in business letters, but it can be used before a direct quotation, instead of a comma. The more usual use for the colon, however, is to introduce a list, examples or explanations, e.g. 'Everyone attending the press preview will be given: a copy of the release, a set of photographs, a wallet of swatches, and a small souvenir.'

Question mark. Otherwise known as the interrogation mark, it is used only after a direct question, never an indirect one, e.g. 'Has John been in yet?' But: 'He asked me whether John had been in.' A question mark can also be used between parentheses to indicate that a word or statement is in doubt, although this is more likely to occur in a memorandum or report than in a letter.

Exclamation mark. Use this very sparingly indeed in a business letter, if at all. It should only be used in genuine exclamations, such as: 'Hello, there!' 'You *are* looking well!' 'Get off that parapet!'. It is sometimes used to indicate that the word or sentence which precedes it is charged with emotion. Some people use the exclamation mark out of sheer exuberance, but it is best to contain yourself, especially in a business letter.

Inverted commas. These are used before and after direct speech. If you are faced with a quotation within a quotation, then you will need to use double inverted commas for the first quotation and single ones within that, or vice versa according to house style. "One of these days," said the M.D., "I shall have to put a notice up saying: 'Keep Out'."

Inverted commas, either single or double, are, of course, also used to enclose titles of plays, songs, operas; names of inns, restaurants, hotels, and a great many other things. In print however, such titles are given in italics and not within inverted commas.

Brackets. The use of the bracket is self-evident. It serves to enclose a brief explanation, a reference or an aside with a secondary bearing on the subject. It is not used very much in business correspondence except for enumerating items, e.g. (1), (2), (3) and so on. If you *do* use brackets, however, you should bear in mind that they are not a substitute for other punctuation marks, but should be inserted where they belong, leaving the existing punctuation as it is. It would be wrong, for instance, to write:

The workers are dispirited and uninterested in their jobs, and are probably thinking , (if they are thinking at all), of other things.

The commas before and after the brackets do not belong there at all, since the brackets adequately enclose the parenthetical statement and if the statement were not there, the sentence would run on without any pause at all.

Hyphen. The hyphen is used to unite two separate words into a compound one. In time, such compound words become one and the hyphen is dropped. The trouble arises with those compound words which are in the last stages of becoming well and truly married into one; some writers will hyphenate them and others will not. The only sensible thing to do in such cases is to decide which course you will take and remain faithful to it. You might decide, for instance, to follow the *Oxford Dictionary for Writers and Editors* or a favourite dictionary of your own and stick to your decision all the time.

Dash. Some people pepper their letters with dashes as a substitute for other punctuation marks. They feel that a pause is called for, they cannot make up their minds whether a stop, a comma or a semicolon will fill the bill, so they pop in a dash and hope for the best. Strictly speaking, a dash should only be used to signify a sudden break in the reasoning, the resumption of a scattered subject, or an omission, such as an oath or the name of someone who for some reason should remain incognito. Here are some examples:

Loyalty, capacity, industry – these are the qualities we seek in our employees.
The report stated mysteriously that the *coup* was masterminded by Colonel –

Be sparing in your use of dashes and before putting one in ask yourself whether a pair of commas or brackets might not serve you equally well.

Forms of address

In using this book, you will be able to read your incoming letter, decide whether it can be answered without fresh composition and if so, select the suitable paragraphs from the chapters which follow, write their identification number on your incoming letter and pass the job on to a typist.

If your office is equipped with a word processor with a suitable storage facility, your operator will already have stored the numbered paragraphs and classified them under the various subject-headings. All she will need to do now is recall the paragraphs you have indicated, edit in any additional details, match in the name and address and present the letters for your signature.

It may not be superfluous to add that it is a good practice to deal with one subject only per letter, even if what you have to say on any one subject is very little. This practice facilitates your own filing and that of your correspondent. Hours are wasted in some offices searching through files for a letter, ultimately to discover that it was filed under a different heading since it dealt with two different subjects.

Strictly speaking all business letters should be addressed to the company, should begin with 'Dear Sirs' and end with 'Yours faithfully'. Nowadays, however, it is far more customary for business people to write to each other as individuals, addressing their letters to: John H. Smith, Esq., or Mrs, Miss, Ms Joan H. Smith. They then begin 'Dear Mr, Mrs, Miss, Ms Smith', as the case may be, or even 'Dear John' or 'Dear Joan', ending their letter with 'Yours sincerely'. 'Esquire' is gradually falling into disuse and certainly one day we shall all follow the American practise of addressing men as plain 'Mr So-and-So'. Do not be in too great a hurry to discard 'Esq.', however, since it appears that men are rather partial to it and it is still firmly entrenched in the professions, the Civil Service and some business houses.

An alternative form is to address your letter to the company and then add, further down: 'Att: Mr, Mrs, Miss or Ms J.W. Weeks'. If you decide to use this form, your opening should still be 'Dear Sirs', since the letter is addressed to the company and not to an individual.

Women usually add 'Mrs, Miss or Ms' after their name when they sign their letters and this enables you to address them in the way they prefer. If no indication is given, then address your letter to 'Ms So-and-So'. Do not, however, use 'Ms' for all women, as a great many of them loathe this form of address and resent having it imposed on them.

If you want to give your business letters a more personal touch, you can 'top and tail' them, that is, write in by hand the 'Dear Mr/Mrs/Miss/Ms So-and-So', the 'Dear Bill', or the 'Dear Joan', as well as the complimentary close. It is amazing how much warmth this practice adds to your letters.

If you sell anything by direct mail you will be sending out hundreds or even thousands of identical letters several times a year. With the facilities available these days there is no longer any excuse for not having a name to go with everyone on your mailing list and, consequently, for not addressing each standard letter individually. You will therefore have no need to use the very formal style 'Dear Sir or Madam'.

Some of your correspondents may have a military rank, a title, degree or letters after their name and you may well be puzzled as to how to address them.

Letters denoting Masters' or Bachelors' degrees, MA, BA, BSc, are rarely used, except when writing to someone in the teaching profession.

Letters standing for membership of learned societies are usually added only if they imply special distinction. You would add FRS (Fellow of the Royal Society), FBA (Fellow of the British Academy), but not F.R.Hist.S (Fellow of the Royal Historical Society) or FRGS (Fellow of the Royal Geographical Society).

Initials indicating professional qualifications or official status should be used only for professional or official correspondence. One exception to this rule is MP, which should follow the name of every Member of Parliament. The other exception is QC (Queen's Counsel).

Honours initials should follow the name. Knights are addressed: Sir John Blank, for a Knight Bachelor, but otherwise followed by the initials of the appropriate order of chivalry. Wives of knights take the title 'Lady', followed by the husband's surname. Dames are addressed as Dame Mary Brown, followed by the initials of the appropriate order. In addressing a knight holding more than one degree in one or more orders of chivalry, show only the senior appointment in each order, e.g. GCVO and not GCVO, KCVO, CVO.

General practitioners and surgeons are both correctly addressed in the same way as ordinary mortals, with their degree letters after their name. However, physicians are frequently given the courtesy title of 'Doctor', whether they actually have an MD or not and it is perfectly in order to address them in a letter as Dr F.R.Brown.

Further forms of address are given in the Appendix.

Part Two
The Instant Letter-Writer

3

Sales Letters

A sales letter is no more and no less than a sales presentation in writing. It is both easier and harder to accomplish than a live presentation. Easier, because you have all the time in the world to think of what you are going to say. Harder, because you cannot gauge your audience reaction as you go along and adjust your story to it. Harder also because a letter going to a number of people, whether a dozen or thousands, must of necessity be more generalized and consequently lose some of its impact.

It follows that you cannot write a good sales letter unless you have first mastered the basic principles of salesmanship. As every salesman worth his salt knows, a customer buys because he is dissatisfied with what he has or because he wants something he does *not* have. Yet he does not simply want a car, he wants comfort, convenience, status. He does not want to own an insurance policy, but he wants safety and security for himself and his family. He – or she – does not want clothes, but rather to attract the opposite sex or maintain the interest of husband or wife.

In other words, customers, or prospective customers, buy the benefits which a product or service brings to them, and it is these benefits which the salesperson and the sales letter have to stress.

These customer benefits, as they are called in marketing parlance, are very closely tied to man's basic needs, the only difference being that in today's world it has become a policy to increase these needs artificially, so that in place of the need for shelter, food, love and security, we now have a 'need' for the latest model refrigerator and the 'need' for a diamond ring, while certain items have become symbols and fulfil quite a different need from the apparent one.

Whether basic or carefully cultivated, however, all these needs boil down to self-interest. Customers are mainly interested in themselves and their family. Not you and your company and your product, but themselves and what needs your product can satisfy.

Your successful salesperson and sales letter will therefore stress customer benefits and will take the 'you' approach. The salesperson's speech and the sales letter will be peppered with 'you's and 'your', while the 'I's and 'we's will be few and far between.

The salesperson's carefully prepared presentation will have but one aim – to make a sale. All the way through his talk, as he steers his prospect from one point to the other, he will have his goal firmly in mind and when he reaches the climax of his argument he will attempt to close the sale, using one of the many techniques at his command. Likewise the sales letter. It should have one aim alone and it should state it clearly and unequivocally.

A tried-and-true American sales formula breaks down into the following stages:

Step 1: Ho Hum! This is the salesperson's opening gambit, designed to wake the audience up, to gain attention, to get through.

Step 2: Why bring that up? Now the salesperson answers the prospect's mental question by pointing out how the proposition will benefit him or her.

Step 3: For instance? The prospect does not take the salesperson's claims at face value and even if he says nothing, he mentally questions his every statement. So in Step 3 the salesperson supports every claim made with specific examples, facts, figures, pictures and so on.

Step 4: So what? Still the prospect questions, and the good salesperson calls for action. He asks for the order. He gets the subscription form signed, or he moves the deal forward to its logical conclusion.

This formula can be followed almost exactly in a sales letter and, in fact, it differs very little from the time-honoured AIDA formula for writing sales letters. The initials stand for:

Attention
Interest
Desire
Action

In other words, every good sales letter should:

1 Gain the reader's *attention*, much as the salesperson's Ho Hum! does.
2 Arouse and hold his *interest*.
3 Kindle his *desire* for the proposition the letter suggests.
4 Urge him to take the *action* the letter suggests.

The opening sentence is the most important one in your whole letter, for if you do not succeed in gaining your reader's attention your whole effort will have been fruitless. Your letter will end in the waste-paper basket, together with countless other circular letters. A business person normally has a pile of letters to read every day. He is busy, pressed for time. He glances at a circular and if nothing in it arrests his attention, he tosses it away without another look.

How are you going to hook him, make him want to read on? You can appeal to his self-interest, give him a piece of shattering news or kindle his curiosity. You can do it either in a regular opening sentence or, better yet, especially in a letter going to business people, by using a headline.

You could, for instance, have a headline saying:

How to increase sales in 1986

or you could vary it in one of several ways:

How YOU can increase sales in 1986
You, too, can increase sales in 1986

If you decide to use a headline opening, then you can proceed right on to your 'I' for interest.

If you decide on an arresting first paragraph, you can use one of several devices:

1 You can launch right in and tell him how your product or service can benefit him.
2 You can get right down to brass tacks and tell him what you want him to do and how this will benefit him.
3 You can flatter him by asking his advice or asking him to do you a favour.
4 You can startle him with a piece of shattering news about a new process or technique.
5 You can give him a bit of useful information about his own business, trade or profession.

Sometimes, you can simply gain a reader's attention by the liveliness of your style and personality, even while you cheerfully ignore all the rules, or most of them, and many of the world's most successful sales letters have been of this rule-breaking sort. It is just as well to bear this constantly in mind.

Having satisfactorily settled the question of 'A' for attention, you are ready to go ahead with stage 2 or 'I' for interest. Make it a short paragraph which follows on smoothly from your headline opener or your first paragraph. It should immediately and satisfactorily answer the questions which are crowding in your reader's mind. 'What *is* this? What will it do for me? Why should I spend my time reading about it?' and similar sentiments.

In other words, your second paragraph should immediately mention the first or most important benefit which your product or service offers. This should arouse your reader's interest and pave the way for your desire-kindling paragraphs, the 'D' of AIDA.

This desire-kindling section of your letter will usually require several paragraphs, but you should strive, none the less, to make your letter as short as possible, for few people have the patience, time or inclination to wade through a letter which goes into a second page.

The golden rule for this section of your letter is: stress customer benefits. Hammer them home. Make your reader dissatisfied with what he has or with doing without. Tell him what your product will do for him, his business, his family, his love life. Play on his emotions. Show enthusiasm. Enthusiasm is like fire. It spreads rapidly.

Don't expect your reader to take your word for what you say. Introduce some proof. A good testimonial or even two are a good idea. But above all – give him reasons why he should buy your product or service. In other words, decide which are the main customer benefits your proposition has to offer and play them for all they're worth.

You are now ready for your final thrust, the one which is to spur your reader on to action – the action *you* want. This action will depend very much on your product. It will not necessarily be a question of his writing out a cheque and ordering your product or a dozen of them. Your proposition may well be one requiring the intervention of your sales representative. In this case the action you want is an appointment for your representative. Or you may want your reader to sign on the dotted line to renew his subscription. You may want him to send for your descriptive booklet or other piece of printed matter.

But whatever the required action is, make quite sure you tell him in unequivocal terms. If you actually want his cheque, your task will be harder and you must try and prise it out of him before his desire for your proposition has cooled down. If you ask him to send in his order and bill him later, you will find him more amenable to persuasion.

If you simply want your correspondent to send for a free booklet or grant you an appointment, your task will be that much simpler, but even so, you should make action as easy for him as possible. Enclose a FREEPOST card or envelope or if you are seeking an appointment, try saying: 'I'll ask my secretary to phone yours for an appointment.'

Whenever possible address your direct sales letters to individuals. In such cases you can begin your letter with 'Dear Mr Brown' or 'Dear Miss Brown'. Nothing has greater impact than the use of a person's name. The advent of the wordprocessor makes it very easy to store your mailing list in the machine's memory and not only run off your envelopes in record-quick time, but also to match in the names and addresses of the addressees, as well as the 'Dear Mr or Miss So-and-So'. Each letter will appear to have been individually typed, thereby gaining enormously in impact.

There will be times when you do not have actual names and in such cases you will have to begin your letter 'Dear Sir or Madam'. A better alternative, where possible, is to write 'Dear Retailer', 'Dear Motorist' or whatever is appropriate.

The opening paragraphs which follow begin in a variety of ways, but they do so in the hope that you will be able to use actual names instead. Paragraphs that belong together and cannot be used alone are given a single number as they should be used as a unit.

Opening paragraphs

1   Dear Sir or Madam,

   Would you like to increase your turnover without tying up additional capital?

   Then why not add our line of ____ to your range of carpets? There are very few quality products which show such excellent profits without tying up capital in stock.

Dear Sir or Madam,

  You, too, can increase your turnover without tying **2**
up additional capital.

  You can do this by becoming an ____ agent and
adding our line of ____ to your range of ____. Very few
products give you such an excellent margin of profit
without the need to tie up precious capital in stock.

Dear Retailer, **3**

   How to increase your turnover without
     typing up further capital

  More and more carpet specialists are realizing the
potential of window furnishings as a complement to their
carpet range and in consequence are becoming agents for
____ roller blinds. Few other products offer such an
excellent profit potential without the need to tie up capital
in stock.

Dear Sir, **4**

   Now you can increase your turnover without
     investing fresh capital

  Sounds incredible? But it's true. You can do just this
by adding our line of ____ to your range of . . . Our two
products complement each other superbly and all you need
to sell our ____ is a couple of square metres of space and
not a penny invested in stock.

Dear Sir or Madam, **5**

   A cure for smoking chimneys

  Now at last you can offer your customers a really
foolproof remedy for their smoking chimneys.

6   Dear Gardening Enthusiast,

Have you ever felt that cultivating your garden is a slow and laborious job and wished you had a magic wand to do it for you in a jiffy?

Well, we cannot go so far as offering you a magic wand, but our newly-developed ____ certainly goes a long way towards it.

7   Dear Motorist,

Have you ever wished you could clean and service your car without getting your hands greasy and grimy?

Our fabulous new ____ has been especially developed to make your wish come true.

8   Dear Sir or Madam,

How to cut costs with corrugated bulk containers

Like all alert shippers, you are no doubt constantly on the look-out for new ways to save money in packaging. Corrugated containers are the answer. They can replace steel drums and many other costly materials and cut down your packaging bills considerably.

9   Dear Sir,

Have you ever stopped to consider how much time and effort are wasted daily at your plant in moving equipment and goods in and out and from one part of the floor to another?

Think of the savings you could effect if the flow of materials were to be studied scientifically and well-designed materials-handling equipment installed.

Dear Investor,   **10**

  Simply fill in the coupon on the enclosed leaflet and
you will receive a copy of ____ to examine at your leisure. If
you do not feel that this book will be invaluable to you in
making future investment decisions, then you can return it
to us and you will be under no obligation whatsoever to buy
it.

Dear Sir or Madam,   **11**

  Would you believe that an able business person could
have a valuable asset without realizing it?

  Well, such is the case if you are unaware that your
employees are your company's most valuable asset.

  If you want to know how to take care of these
valuable assets, send for a copy of ____ today.

Dear Sir or Madam,   **12**

  Don't let spring catch you unawares. Phone right
away to 602-6481 and arrange to have your premises
redecorated while we still have some free dates on our
calendar.

Dear Sir or Madam,   **13**

  If you will please sign and return to us the enclosed
special-offer form you will receive, absolutely free, a copy of
____, which we are sending to all our clients to celebrate
our 25th anniversary.

Dear Sir,   **14**

<u>Are your profits going down the drain?</u>

  . . . . . just trickling away through the use of
antiquated tools which waste time, need frequent
maintenance, and do a slow inadequate job?

  Surely it is time to stop this drain on profits?

15   Dear Reader,

We know how busy you are and hate to trouble you, but we <u>do</u> need your help and feel sure you will be kind enough to co-operate. What we should like are the names of up to a dozen business people like yourself whom you feel would benefit from reading ____ every month as you do. May we ask you to write down the names and addresses on the enclosed form and return it to us in the accompanying envelope?

In return for your help we shall send you a Business Person's Desk Book for 1986 in a very special edition prepared exclusively for our subscribers.

16   Dear Sir or Madam,

Did you know you could cut your lighting costs by switching to ____ lamps?

____ lamps save you money in two ways: first of all, they stay bright longer than any other lamp and, secondly, they save you the time and manpower needed to keep cleaning them, as you have to with other lamps.

17   Dear Sir or Madam,

<u>How to cut down on transport costs</u>

Have you ever stopped to consider how heavily transport impinges on your profit margin?

We have – and, in consequence, we have drawn up a complete plan which over a period will save you pounds.

18   Dear Sir,

How many work-hours did you lose last year through letting your operatives make do with inadequate safety equipment?

One operative off the job for a day will cost you more in hard cash than an adequate pair of goggles or safety shoes, quite apart from humanitarian considerations.

Dear Sir or Madam,   **19**

     Want to double your production, cut your costs by 30
per cent and install complete quality-control in one fell
swoop?

     Then scrap your antiquated ____ and switch to ____.

Dear Sir or Madam,   **20**

<u>How to double your production without
increasing overheads</u>

     It sounds almost too good to be true. Yet it <u>is</u> true.
All you need do is pension off your ____ system and install
the fully automatic ____.

Dear Sir,   **21**

     Productivity problem?

     We cannot claim to solve all of them, but certainly
our ____ is the answer to a good many.

Dear Sir or Madam,   **22**

     Do you ever have a display problem?

     Then let ____ solve it for you – simply, beautifully,
economically and completely.

Dear Builder,   **23**

<u>The luxury touch which increases your profits</u>

     Like all builders, you are no doubt anxious to add
that extra touch of luxury to your houses which results in a
higher selling-price. But you don't want the luxury to cost
<u>you</u> too much and we don't blame you.

     To meet this special need of yours we have brought
out a special contract model of our popular ____. It still
gives the luxury touch, but is not so hard on the pocket.

24   Dear Sir or Madam,

Do you prefer Yes-men to Know-men?

If so, you'll not be needing our services, since we have not a single Yes-man on our team of creative copywriters, visualisers and artists.

25   Dear Madam,

Off to the beach? Then you'll need a 'shore winner' in your suitcase. Every single swimsuit in our summer collection is just that.

26   Dear Sir or Madam,

You may have heard about a very famous maker of electrical appliances who recently came to grief. We won't mention his name – he's embarrassed enough already – but we know you know whom we mean.

Well, it happens that the ill wind which swept him away enabled us to buy a very large consignment of ____ at an unusually low price and we would now like you to share our good fortune and get yourself one at a price never before heard of.

27   Dear Madam,

As a special introduction to our new Salon de Coiffure, Monsieur Henri will be with us in person from our Paris headquarters during the whole of next week.

If you act now you can have a completely new hair style created for you by this inimitable artist, who dresses the hair of some of the most beautiful women in the world.

28   Dear Customer,

Dry cleaning in the middle of summer ? Why not, if you can get the job done at a considerable saving ? From now until July 15 all dry cleaning jobs will be carried out at 25 per cent less than the normal price.

Dear Sir,   29

      Thousands need us for our shelves alone.

      How about you? Have you no storage or display
problems? If you have, why not let us solve them for you?

Dear Sir or Madam,   30

      Is it an internal natter ?

      Then keep your telephone lines clear and install a
____ internal communications unit instead.

Dear Sir,   31

      Once upon a time an engineer needed an air-operated
remote control valve and found out that ____ made just
what he needed. Later on he wanted a mechanical trip valve
and discovered that ____ supplied those too.

      His various jobs always seemed to require some sort
of valve or other and every time he found that ____ could
give him what he wanted. Do you wonder that he is now
living happily ever after with ____ valves?

Dear Sir or Madam,   32

      Worried by shortage of skilled staff? Rising
overheads? Cut-throat competition?

      Put your mind at ease and let ____ solve all three
problems at once.

Dear Sir or Madam,   33

      Are you always asking the impossible?

      That certainly won't worry us – the impossible is
routine with ____.

34   Dear Sir or Madam,

Do you have all the facts at your fingertips?

Impossible? Certainly not. Not with ____.

35   Dear Sir,

Did you read about the company which saved £22,500 a year by cutting down 20 people and got more speed and efficiency into the bargain?

Like to hear how you can do the same for <u>your</u> company?

36   Dear Sir or Madam,

Don't move to the moon if you need more space.

Let us show you how to make the most of the space you've got!

37   Dear Sales Manager,

Would you like ____ to keep her eye on your sales force?

She will immediately be able to spot anyone who's falling behind target.

But that's not all that ____ can do.

The body of the letter

First of all, our wholesale prices are very **38**
competitive, leaving you plenty of leeway for a substantial
margin of profit.

Secondly, our range of ____ complement your own
products most admirably. In fact, our handsome ____ should
almost sell themselves, since a customer coming into the
store to buy a new ____ will almost certainly be interested
in other items for the home as well.

____ Limited of ____ are one firm who realized the
possibilities which our products offered. In the first year
alone they sold ____ of them, which brought them a net
profit of ____. This year, they feel sure they will be able to
double these figures – and all without adding one more
penny to the business!

The ____ is child's play to install, needs absolutely no **39**
maintenance and can be counted on to last for many years.

As if this were not enough, it will only cost your
customers about ____, leaving you a very handsome margin,
since we sell the ____ to you at £____ a hundred.

We have literally thousands of satisfied users and can
give you actual references to mention to your customers.

The product is advertised both in the National Press **40**
and the women's magazines and the hundreds of inquiries
which pour in to us daily are immediately passed on to our
dealers.

As you may have noticed, our products are advertised **41**
extensively with the result that our retailers' selling is
already partly done for them.

42   One of our new customers, ____ of ____, used to ship
their chemicals in steel drums and their annual bill for
packaging was usually in the region of £____. For the past
year they have switched to our ____ corrugated box with its
polyethylene lining, saving themselves no less than £____
in packaging bills.

          Our ____ box gives perfect protection to ____'s
product and we have other boxes which would suit your
products equally well. Why indulge in the extravagance of
steel drums when corrugated boxes do the job equally well
and cost you less than half?

43   A word from you and our engineers will move in and
make a careful study of your operation, followed by
recommendations on the equipment you need to streamline
the flow of materials in your plant.

          The net result? Increased productivity, higher
personnel morale, greater safety, more efficiency – all of
which, you will readily agree, spell greater profits for your
company.

44   How to decide how much the stock is really worth,
how to improve your timing, how to read the charts, how to
recognize the technical signals – these are some of the
things this valuable book will tell you.

          Yet this is not all; every one of the book's twenty
chapters is jam-packed with useful information for the
investor. Whether you own ten common stocks or ten
thousand, this book will help you to become a better
investor, will show you how to make your money work
harder for you.

45   Our team of painters and decorators works quietly
and unobtrusively, so that you and your staff will hardly
know they're there. Neither will our bill upset your
exchequer unduly. Yet think of the advantages of freshly
decorated offices! Staff morale rises sky high, customers are
impressed, the premises are given a new lease of life,
accidents and boredom are reduced – all this for the price of
a new coat of paint!

Let our company take the whole problem off your **46**
shoulders and advise you on the correct safety equipment
for your particular operation. Our experts are only too
eager to serve you and we have a complete range of safety
equipment for every industrial situation.

Remember – accidents increase production costs,
lower morale, waste time and materials. It's good business
to get good safety equipment for your employees. ____ brand
is the best.

In fact, ____ make hundreds of types of valves and **47**
every one of them meets the highest standard of reliability.
Whether you need a valve to restrict, direct, stop, delay or
regulate; a manual, mechanical or remote control valve ____
are the people to go to. We make the valves with your
problems in mind.

Designed with you in mind, every one of our **48**
swimsuits is guaranteed to flatter your figure and attract
admiring glances. The colours are delightful, the cut superb,
the fit perfect.

The answer is Graphbox. Smaller even than a **49**
portable typewriter, this little miracle of modern technology
can actually draw your graphs for you at the touch of a few
keys.

Line graphs, bar graphs, pie charts, each complete
with hatchings of various sorts – Graphbox can handle
them all. And anyone on your staff, without any special
training, can handle Graphbox.

For the modest outlay of £____ you can save your
staff many hours of toil at the drawing board, with
resultant savings for you.

Easy to install and take down, perfectly adaptable to **50**
a variety of different situations, bang up to date in
appearance, incredibly strong and long-wearing, the ____
display units are indeed the answer to a display person's
problems.

51   The benefits offered by the ____ Wordprocessor are
legion, and this is no exaggeration. It will turn out at speed
letters of impeccable appearance which will greatly
enhance your company's image. Yet the ____ Wordprocessor
is very much more than a glorified typewriter. With the aid
of the appropriate printer it will produce all your mailing
shots at the touch of a button and match-in the addresses to
perfection. Press another button and the ____ will produce
the envelopes to complete the mailing.

Standard paragraphs or clauses can be stored in the
____'s memory for insertion at will into letters or
documents.

Writing those difficult reports will be greatly
simplified, as your secretary will no longer have to re-type
draft after draft. The editing function in your Wordprocessor
will permit her simply to 'key-in' the changes you require
and return the document to you for further study.

52   The ____ range of visible records gives you all the
facts at a glance – simply, accurately, speedily.

Whether you are interested in quick and efficient
control of sales, stocks, purchasing, production or ledgers,
the ____ system is the answer.

53   ____ can also take care of your invoicing and stock
control. As the invoice is produced, the stock is
automatically up-dated. This means, of course, that ____
carries out two very important tasks almost
simultaneously, not to mention various smaller tasks which
the machine can carry out in its spare time.

54   Consider the facts: all you need do is make a drill or
shallow trench with the hoe, sprinkle a handful of ____ into
it and sow your seeds on top. No digging, no cultivating at
all. ____ will do the work for you, gradually breaking down
the soil into a porous, friable loam.

55   Why not come in and see them for yourself?

Closing paragraphs

We look forward to seeing you soon. Do hurry before **56**
all the best numbers have gone.

Why not send for a trial bag right away? **57**

Our technical representative will be in your area **58**
soon and will phone for an appointment. He will be happy
to give you complete details of the ____ without any
obligation whatsoever on your part.

Why not phone ____ and ask for our technical **59**
representative to come along and give you more complete
details?

The ____ is available now at all electricity **60**
showrooms. Why not go into your nearest one and see a
demonstration of this remarkable machine?

May we bring a ____ along to show you? Our **61**
representative will be in your area next week and will
phone for an appointment.

If you will kindly return the enclosed card to us, we **62**
will send our representative along as quickly as possible.

Hadn't you better get in touch with us soon? **63**

Why not let ____ increase your turnover, too? Our **64**
representative will be in touch with you soon.

Better get a copy now. **65**

66   Please use the enclosed reply card. It won't commit you in any way and may lead to greater speed and efficiency in your company.

67   Why not get your secretary to give us a ring? We'll be happy to come along and explain to you in more detail how ____ can save your company pounds.

68   May I come along and tell you more about our service?

69   Why not make a general turn-out and bring your clothes in to be cleaned today? Remember – our special offer is open only until July 15.

70   But remember – Monsieur Henri will be here only for a week. Don't miss your chance. Come along right away.

71   Samples are available on request without obligation. Write today.

72   Don't delay. Act now. Just fill in the bottom portion of this letter and return it to us in the enclosed envelope. We will do the rest.

73   Send for a supply at once, before our stocks run out. You'll be glad you did so.

74   Like to see a demonstration of the ____ right in your own office? Then complete the enclosed reply card and we shall be happy to arrange it.

4

Acknowledging Orders and Suggestions

Business people will not quarrel with the statement that getting an order is the most important event of the day. Bigger and better orders are their dream. If orders don't keep on coming in they will soon be out of business. Yet do they always show proper appreciation to customers? Do you, for instance?

The first and most obvious requirement is to acknowledge every order received, preferably on the same day. If your business is the kind which gets a small number of large orders, rather than thousands of small ones, then you will certainly be well advised to acknowledge each order with an individual letter. Many large companies, however, especially if they habitually receive a great number of orders, have to resort to an acknowledgment postcard or printed form letter, and in many instances this is a perfectly adequate solution.

Now that the use of the electronic typewriter is becoming more widespread, however, many more companies could send out a personalized acknowledgment and, unquestionably, their customer relations would be all the better for it.

The kind of acknowledgment you write will depend, of course, on your type of business and the kind of orders you receive. Alert retailers will, for instance, write a 'thank you' letter to a customer who has been in to make his or her first purchase since opening a charge account. All that is required in such cases is to say 'thank you', welcome the customer to the 'club', make him or her feel satisfied with the wisdom of the purchase and, if appropriate, enclose a piece of literature which might inspire a further purchase. In short, this type of acknowledgment is purely a goodwill message, an exercise in customer relations. Select appropriate letters from the pages which follow, commit them to your wordprocessor's memory and use and re-use them at the touch of a few keys.

If the order has yet to go off, your acknowledgment should serve the additional purpose of telling the customer when to expect the merchandise ordered. This occurs, of course, in the case of a manufacturer or wholesaler, or indeed any company selling by direct mail.

Be sure, therefore, to mention the approximate date of dispatch and how the merchandise will be sent. If you can only make a part-shipment, make

51

this clear in your acknowledgment, since you will antagonize your customer by shipping half the order without a word of explanation. Similarly, if you cannot ship reasonably quickly, some explanation is needed. Try to make your customer feel that the balance of the order is well worth waiting for.

In the unfortunate event of your not being able to ship the style or pattern ordered at all, suggest a substitute and do all you can to persuade your customer that it will fill the need as well as, if not better than, what he or she originally ordered. Do not send a substitute without permission, unless there has been an agreement to that effect.

Often you will have to pass the order on to another branch, or to the dealer in the customer's area, or otherwise have someone else fill the order. In such cases, you will obviously mention this in your acknowledgment letter, sending a carbon to the branch or dealer concerned.

Quite frequently a customer will not give you sufficient information to enable you to fill the order. He will omit size, colour, calibre, voltage or other essential details. When writing back, make it as easy as possible for your customer to give you the required information.

Acknowledging suggestions

Customers and individual users of your products will sometimes send in suggestions of all sorts. Whether good, bad or indifferent, every suggestion must be acknowledged and proper appreciation shown for the trouble taken to think up the idea and write and tell you about it.

The two cardinal rules, therefore, in dealing with suggestions from customers and users are: (1) acknowledge promptly, and (2) show due appreciation. What you say after that will depend rather on the nature of the suggestion and whether you plan to try it or not. Needless to say, you will have to display considerable tact when dealing with hare-brained suggestions.

Some cases call for the advice of your legal department and any letter claiming compensation for a suggestion used or assumed to have been used should be promptly turned over to your legal advisers.

Opening paragraphs – orders

75   Dear Mrs Jones,

We were delighted to welcome you to the store yesterday when you made your first purchases since opening your charge account.

Dear Ms Hudson,   **76**

   Thank you for coming to White's yesterday and
making your first purchase as an account customer.

Dear Miss Simpson,   **77**

   We should like you to know how much we
appreciated your visit yesterday when you made your first
purchase on your new charge account.

Dear Sirs,   **78**

   Our sincere thanks for your opening order. We
certainly appreciate your interest in our products and this
opportunity of being of service to you.

Dear Mr Brown,   **79**

   Welcome to our rapidly increasing family of ____
owners. Your service book is enclosed. You will see from the
first page that you are entitled to a free service at 500
miles, so we look forward to seeing you again then.

Dear Ms King,   **80**

   Welcome to the vast and happy family of ____
owners, and thank you for returning your warranty card.
As you will have gathered from the card, your ____ is
guaranteed for ____ years from any defect in workmanship
and materials.

Dear Sirs,   **81**

   Many thanks for your first order. We very much look
forward to being of service to you and appreciate your
interest in our products.

82   Dear Sirs,

It is a pleasure to welcome you to the large and growing group of ____ customers. You may be sure that your first order, received this morning, will have our careful and prompt attention.

83   Dear Sirs,

We were delighted to receive your first order this morning and consider it a privilege to do business with your company.

84   Dear Sirs,

Thank you for your first order, received today. It is indeed a pleasure to welcome you as a new customer and we look forward to doing business with you.

85   Dear Ms Wade,

Your Order No. ____ dated July 28

Our sincere thanks for your order received today.

86   Dear Mr Wells,

Your Order No. ____ dated March 23

You will be pleased to learn that your order for ____ is already in hand.

87   Dear Ms Squires,

Ceiling roses

Thank you for your Order No. ____ dated June 16.

Opening paragraphs – suggestions

Dear Ms Barrows,   **88**

    Thank you for your most constructive suggestion regarding the shape of our ____ carton.

Dear Mr White,   **89**

    It was indeed good of you to go to the trouble of writing to us about our advertising.

Dear Mr Whitman,   **90**

    Thank you for your letter of June 10 in which you suggest improvements in the closing of our ____ tins.

Dear Mrs Gilmore,   **91**

    We are most grateful for your letter of April 23 in which you suggest several different ways in which our ____ could be used.

The body of the letter – orders

    We feel quite confident that you will be more than   **92**
satisfied with the ____ you selected and look forward to the pleasure of serving you for many years to come.

    We feel sure you will find this way of shopping very   **93**
convenient and trouble-free and we look forward to seeing you in the store often.

    The enclosed booklet will help you to find your way   **94**
around the store and give you some indication of the many other things which ____'s has to offer.

95   The ___ will go out by our own van on January 30 and this will be the date on our invoice. Since this is your first order, you will no doubt be interested to know what our terms are. There is a 3 per cent discount for payment within ten days of invoice date, and 1 per cent for payment within 30 days, the invoice amount being due net thereafter.

We feel sure you will want to take advantage of this opportunity of making extra profit on our line of ___.

96   The ___ will go out to you by parcel post early next week and should therefore reach you in plenty of time for your needs.

As this is the first occasion on which we have had the pleasure of dealing with your company, we think you may be interested to learn that our terms are ___. Many of our long-standing customers take advantage of our generous terms to make additional profits on our ___.

97   We are putting your order into production immediately and will advise you of the shipping date as soon as possible.

98   The ___ ordered can be sent to you immediately from stock and will be despatched by ___ on January 21.

99   We make two deliveries a week in your area and are hoping to include the ___ ordered in our Thursday's trip.

100   Your order will be shipped by British Rail at the end of next week.

101   We note that you wish to pick the goods up yourself and will have them ready for you by ___ as you request.

102   The goods will be sent by first available flight and we will let you have further details soon.

We will airfreight the order, as requested, within a   **103**
few days.

It will be despatched within ten to fifteen days by   **104**
___.

Since all our orders for the West Country are handled   **105**
by our Bristol branch, we are sending your order on to
Bristol and you will be hearing from them soon.

We are sending your order on to our ___ dealer, as   **106**
he handles all our business in your area. No doubt you will
be hearing from him soon.

To get the merchandise off to you with the least   **107**
possible delay, we are sending your order to our Glasgow
branch, which normally deals with all business for
Scotland.

You will be pleased to learn that your order will go   **108**
out to you within the next two weeks from our ___
warehouse.

The model installed is the very latest and we have   **109**
every confidence that it will give you long and satisfactory
service. Be sure to read the operating and maintenance
instructions booklet which our fitter left with the ___. You
will find it both useful and instructive.

We are quite sure you will be more than satisfied   **110**
with your beautiful new ___. Not only is it the very latest
in design, but, perhaps even more important, it
incorporates all the most up-to-date technical advances. It
is a ___ you can really be proud to show your friends.

111   After you have been using it for some time, we should be very interested to learn your impressions. Our customers' ideas and suggestions help us to improve our products all the time and to make sure we are giving them what they want.

Why not jot down your comments on the back of this letter and return it to us in the enclosed envelope?

112   Meanwhile we wish you 'Happy Motoring', secure in the knowledge that you have just acquired the finest small car on the market.

113   The following items will go out to you by ____ early next week:

. . . .
. . . .
. . . .

Unfortunately, however, we are not able to ship items 4 and 5 on your order until early March. We sincerely hope that this will not inconvenience you too much.

114   Every item on your order except No. 3 will be shipped to you from stock within the next couple of days. The 'Camelot', however, will be delayed somewhat. We have had a tremendous demand for this pattern, so much so, in fact, that we have been caught unprepared. Do be assured that we are doing everything we can to catch up with demand and that you will receive your supply as soon as possible.

We are confident that you will find the 'Camelot' pattern every bit as popular with your own customers and that they will feel it was well worth waiting for.

Unfortunately, however, we have to disappoint you **115** this time and cannot promise you delivery until the end of September. The dock strike meant that our raw materials were sitting at Tilbury instead of moving into our works and our production schedules have been seriously upset.

We are sorry indeed to have to inconvenience you in this way, as we are always most anxious to give our customers the best possible service. Owing to the rather unusual circumstances, however, we feel confident that you will bear with us on this occasion.

Regrettably, we are unable to meet your requested **116** delivery date. The response to our new spring range has been so overwhelming that we are having difficulty in keeping up with demand. However, we are working two shifts and are very hopeful of being able to make delivery around the end of next month.

Please accept our most sincere apologies for this delay. We feel sure that when you see how rapidly our attractive new models disappear from your racks you will agree that the wait has been worthwhile.

We regret to have to inform you, however, that the **117** model you have chosen is not one we normally carry in stock. We have ordered it from our Danish suppliers and are confident of being able to deliver it to you around the middle of February.

We are sorry to have to keep you waiting for your desk, but are quite sure that when you see its handsome lines and the beautiful grain of the wood and when you begin to see how practical it is in use, you will not regret the long wait.

118   Before we can ship your order we need to have the following information:

1. Colour required
2. Length of pull cord required.

Perhaps you will be good enough to fill in the details alongside and return this letter to us in the enclosed envelope. The accompanying leaflet will refresh your memory as to the colours we can supply.

119   Will you kindly let us know whether you prefer chrome or brass rings, as you do not mention this in your order? As soon as we have this additional information, we will despatch the complete order by our own van.

120   Unfortunately you omitted to indicate the width of rail you require. If you will kindly clarify this detail we will have the rails sent off to you without delay.

121   To supply you with the exact ____ you need for the job, we require some additional information about your operation. The enclosed leaflet indicates the measurements and other details we need and if you will kindly fill it in where appropriate and return it to us in the enclosed envelope we shall be happy to fill your order accordingly.

122   Unfortunately, we no longer manufacture the Model 106M. It has been replaced by the ultimate in ____ which we call the 107. It is not only faster than the 106M, but has a more up-to-date appearance and is easier to clean and maintain.

The price is the same, but performance and appearance have improved. May we send you this extra special ____?

However, the fabric you order is no longer available. **123**
It was discontinued at the end of the spring, to be replaced
by a wealth of wonderful new designs in a variety of
sizzling colours.

We are enclosing swatches of all the new designs in
the green and yellow shades you chose and look forward to
hearing which one of them you prefer.

Unfortunately Investing for Growth is now out of **124**
print and we are not contemplating a new edition. We have,
however, recently published several other excellent books
on the same subject and are enclosing leaflets about them
as well as our current book list.

We look forward to hearing whether we may send
you one of these other books instead.

Regrettably, we are unable to fill your order for ____. **125**
They have been replaced for some time by high-speed
electronic ____. As you can imagine they do the job far more
quickly and accurately than the old ____ and their small
additional cost is amply made up for by the increase in
productivity they generate.

May we ship the new electronic ____ to you?

Although I have not yet had the pleasure of meeting **126**
you, I want you to know that we are here to serve you. If
there is anything I can do to help in any way, do please let
me know.

Do be assured that all of us here will do our utmost **127**
to give you the prompt and efficient service you have a
right to expect. I very much look forward to meeting you
personally next time I am in ____, but if there is anything I
can do to help in the meantime, do please let me know.

The body of the letter – suggestions

128   We are keeping your suggestions by us until we next consider the packaging problem. As you can well imagine, a great many other changes are involved once the shape of a carton is altered and a company does not undertake such changes lightly.

Having thoughtful and imaginative customers like you helps us tremendously in continuing to improve both our product and its packaging.

129   When we plan our next advertising campaign we shall certainly keep your suggestions in mind and are most grateful for your thoughtfulness.

130   As a matter of fact, we have had something rather similar in mind for a long time and when our next advertising campaign breaks you will notice points of similarity between our ideas and your own.

It makes us especially proud to know that some of our customers care enough about us and our products to take time to think so creatively and so intelligently about our problems.

131   We are passing your helpful suggestions on to our research and development department and you will no doubt soon be hearing from Mr John Brown, our Development Engineer.

132   The various ideas you put forward are most ingenious and we should be happy to send them to the press, as you suggest. We should point out, however, that editors are not in the habit of paying for such items. Some magazines do send a small cheque for the 'Letters to the Editor' they publish and if this is what you have in mind, we suggest you look out for a magazine which publishes the 'useful hint' type of letter and send in your suggestions direct.

Closing paragraphs – orders

We hope you will come in again soon and can assure **133**
you that you will be most welcome.

A cordial welcome always awaits you at ____'s and **134**
every member of the staff is eager to serve you and make
your every visit a pleasure.

We are confident you will find our products the finest **135**
on the market and that they will prove a valuable addition
to your present lines. We hope this will prove to be the
beginning of a long and mutually profitable business
relationship.

It is our policy to supply the best possible **136**
merchandise at the most competitive prices compatible
with quality and we also take special pride in assisting our
customers in every way we can.

Do, therefore, let us know if you have any questions
or problems with which you feel we may be able to help.

We look forward to hearing from you. **137**

If you have any questions or if there is some **138**
comment you would like to make on the ____, do drop us a
line. We are genuinely interested in hearing what our
customers think of our products, since it helps us to
continue giving them what they want.

If, on the other hand, you have a friend who might be
interested in getting descriptive literature, perhaps you
would be good enough to send us his or her name and
address.

Thank you again. **139**

140   Thank you again for your initial order which will be sent to you by ___ towards the end of next week.

141   Again, many thanks for the privilege of doing business with you.

142   It is our constant aim to give our customers the best possible service and we certainly hope you will enjoy doing business with us.

Closing paragraphs – suggestions

143   Again, many thanks.

144   In the meantime, thank you for your constructive suggestions.

145   Thank you again for taking the time and trouble to write to us about our product.

146   Do let us know what you have decided to do about your various ideas. Meanwhile, we should like you to know how very much we appreciate loyal and thoughtful customers such as yourself. It is they who help us to make our products the best on the market.

147   Do be assured that we are very grateful for your suggestions and are glad that you wrote to us.

148   It was most thoughtful of you to write and we greatly appreciate it.

5

'Covering' Letters

This chapter is concerned with the type of letter which accompanies shipping documents, *proforma* invoices, estimates, quotations, catalogues or other printed matter, and samples. Some answers to general enquiries are also included.

All these letters fall into one of two categories:

1 The covering letter proper, which accompanies documents. This type of letter needs to be brief, accurate, and complete. Especially where export is concerned, it is extremely important not only to supply all documents exactly as requested by the overseas customer and according to the regulations prevailing in his country, but also to list them carefully in your covering letter. A great deal of time can be wasted by omitting a document, or failing to mention it in your covering letter.

2 The letter giving an estimate or quotation, or enclosing printed matter in answer to a request. This type of letter does not merely 'accompany' a catalogue or quotation, but has a regular selling job to do. It should not limit itself to giving the addressee the information he or she asked for, but should heighten his or her desire for the proposition in question.

In writing this second type of letter you would do well to:

1 Write promptly, if possible the same day that you receive the enquiry.

2 Thank your correspondent for writing, or otherwise show appreciation.

3 Answer *all* your correspondent's questions, not only the first two. Answer them all and answer them completely.

4 Remove any further doubts which may be lingering at the back of your correspondent's mind. Ask yourself what *you* would want to know about your product or service if you were on the outside and then clarify those points in your letter.

5 Be concise. It is quite possible to answer all questions and clarify all doubtful points and yet to do so concisely.

6 Adapt your answer to your writer's needs. Nothing is more infuriating to someone having written in on a certain point, than to feel that the answer is vague and general.

All the above points obviously apply equally to letters written in answer to a

65

general enquiry. On the other hand, there are innumerable cases where all you need do is to say you are enclosing the requested booklet, offer any further assistance which may be needed and then bow out. Such would be the case if, for instance, you made available to the general public a booklet or leaflet of some sort, such as recipes, tips on grooming, desk diaries and so on.

Opening paragraphs

149   Dear Sirs,

Your Order No. . . .

   With reference to the above order, we are now happy to enclose the following documents:

   (1) Invoice No. . . . in triplicate, as requested
   (2) Clean On Board Bill of Lading No. . . .
   (3) Insurance Certificate No. . . .
   (4) Certificate of Origin No. . . .

150   Dear Sirs,

Soc. An. Mario Bianchi, Milan
Their Order No. . . .

   We are enclosing the following documents relating to the above order:

   (1) Irrevocable Letter of Credit No. . . .
   (2) Full Set of Clean On Board Bill of Lading No. . . .
   (3) Insurance Certificate No. . . .
   (4) Certificate of Origin No. . . .
   (5) X copies of Invoice No. . . .

151   Dear Sirs,

The XYZ Company Ltd., Bali
Their Order No. . . .

   We are pleased to enclose the following documents relating to the above order:

   (1) Postal receipt dated January 17, 1985
   (2) Insurance Certificate No. . . .
   (3) Our Invoice No. . . . in quadruplicate
   (4) Consular Invoice No. . . .
   (5) (Any other document enclosed)

Dear Mr. Cook,   **152**

     The enclosed vade-mecum goes to you with our
compliments.

Dear Sirs,   **153**

<u>Your Order No. . . .</u>

     We are pleased to enclose the following documents
relating to the above order:

     (1) Invoice No. . . . in quintuplicate (or as relevant)
     (2) Clean on Board Bill of Lading No. . . .
     (3) Insurance Certificate No. . . .

Dear Sirs,   **154**

<u>Pelleting Plant</u>

     Further to our discussion during your visit to our
works, we are now pleased to enclose Pro-forma Invoice No.
10625 detailing all the material required to set up a
complete pelleting plant in your country, together with
detailed layout of the proposed plant on your premises.

Dear Mr Jones,   **155**

     Enclosed is my estimate for the work you want done
in your garden.

Dear Sirs,   **156**

     We are giving you hereunder our quotation for the
special cardboard boxes you require:

     10 cm x 10 cm x 10 cm £____ per 1000
     15 cm x 15 cm x 15 cm £____ per 1000
     20 cm x 20 cm x 20 cm £____ per 1000

157   Dear Ms Weldon,

I have carefully studied your requirements and give you hereunder what I believe to be a very competitive quotation for the ____ you require:

_____

_____

158   Dear Ms Martin,

We are happy to enclose a copy of our booklet 'The Electronic Office', as you request.

159   Dear Mr Barrett,

Enclosed is a copy of the booklet 'Talking to Your Computer' which you requested.

160   Dear Mr Harrison,

With the enclosed refill for your ____ calendar go our very best wishes for 1986.

161   Dear Mrs Young,

We are pleased to enclose a leaflet on the ____ chair, together with swatches of the coverings available.

162   Dear Mrs Greene,

Thank you for your enquiry. As you request, we are enclosing full details of the ____ range of sun lamps for home use.

163   Dear Mr MacVey,

Thank you for your letter of January 15. We can best reply by enclosing a leaflet which gives complete details on Western Red Cedar Weatherboarding, including the various ways of treating it.

Dear Sirs,   **164**

    We are pleased to enclose our estimate for the
extension to your factory, as requested.

Dear Sirs,   **165**

    With further reference to our letter of March 23, we
are now happy to enclose Pro Forma Invoice No. L.55 in
quadruplicate for the machinery and Pro Forma Invoice No.
L.56 for the tools.

Dear Mrs Griffiths,   **166**

    In reply to your letter of March 21, you will be
pleased to learn that it is indeed possible for you to have a
spit added to your Model 62 ____ cooker.

Dear Mrs White,   **167**

    Thank you for your letter of February 2. We quite
understand your anxiety to keep your lovely new Venetian
blinds as fresh and clean as they were when they first went
up and are happy to assure you that this can be done with
ease.

The body of the letter

    This order was shipped by M.V. 'Merchant   **168**
Adventurer' on September 22.

    Would you kindly collect the amount of £ . . . in cash   **169**
from XYZ Company Ltd in exchange for the enclosed
documents, crediting our account with the proceeds.

    Please collect the invoice amount against the   **170**
enclosed L/C on our behalf.

171   As you will see, we have quoted you CIF prices in Uruguayan Pesos, as you requested, and we sincerely hope that you will have no difficulty in securing the necessary import licence from your Government.

172   Once you have secured the import licence for the material, we shall return to the question of supplying a technical man to help you get the plant into production, but you will no doubt agree that it is wiser to overcome the licence hurdle first of all.

173   We have tried to comply in every way with your instructions in order to reduce the import formalities and sincerely hope that your application will be successful.

174   If we have your acceptance within the next few days, we can certainly finish the work by Easter, as you desire. As mentioned to you on the telephone, we can do the job without the slightest interference to your operation and with very little inconvenience to your staff.

We have in the past carried out quite a number of similar jobs to the complete satisfaction of our clients. One in particular might interest you – the extension to the premises of Woods and Woods, your neighbours in Elizabeth Road. We have spoken to Mr John Woods Senior and he would be very pleased for you to look over the premises at any time. If you care to accept his invitation, you should ring him on 380-6581.

175   As you will see, I have given three alternatives for the path, since the difference in price between a simple hoggin path and crazy paving bedded in concrete is quite large and when you come to consider the whole of the work to be done it will help you to have these alternatives.

As you may imagine, I am extremely busy at this time of the year and I would urge you to let me have your decision as soon as you possibly can so that I can fit the work in before the end of the season.

The prices quoted are for two-tone boxes exactly like **176**
the Japanese sample you sent us. You will readily
understand that such boxes are somewhat laborious to
make and consequently rather more costly than a simpler
design. Should you decide to settle for one of our standard
'cubes' we can give you a far more interesting price.

Delivery on the ____ is from stock and we could **177**
therefore give you very prompt service indeed.

Since the ____ will have to be especially made, **178**
delivery would be around six weeks from receipt of order.

The ____ would be custom-made for you, as you **179**
realize, but we would get them into production as soon as
we receive your order and delivery could be arranged within
two to three weeks later.

We suggest you let us have your order as soon as **180**
possible since, as you know, our busiest season is now upon
us and we are most anxious to meet the delivery date you
mentioned.

As for delivery, we would have no difficulty in **181**
meeting the date you mention.

I am quite confident I can fit your work in this **182**
season, but you should not delay in letting me have your
decision.

We hope you will find it useful. **183**

We have endeavoured to include in it all the **184**
information a business person needs, but does not always
have at hand. We hope that you will find it an indispensable
companion.

185   Designed for out-of-office use, we sincerely hope it will go with you everywhere and prove as useful as its compilers intended it to be.

186   The booklet will explain to you in down-to-earth terms just how the office of the future will work, so you are ready for it when it comes.

187   Many executives are a little awed by computers and the enclosed booklet was prepared to make them more at ease with the subject and to enable them to talk knowledgeably with the experts.

188   It is a year we look forward to very eagerly since we feel it will be a significant one for us. Work on our latest extension is now finished and this almost doubles our production capacity. This means not only that we shall be able to give you better service than ever, but that we are now in a position to accept any job from you, however large.

     In fact, we can now carry out any ____ work for you, since we have both the production capacity and the skilled people to go with it.

189   The chair is designed to support the body in all the right places and you will find that ten minutes in the ____ is almost like a beauty treatment.

     You can sit or recline in the chair in any of five positions and these are selected simply by moving the knob you see on the right. You can do it as you recline without any strain at all.

     In addition, the chair rests on the floor at either of two different angles, which means that you can sit up to read a book or sew, for instance, and then recline right back with your legs in the highest position for perfect relaxation – all without getting up.

     If you want to store the chair away, it folds very easily into a compact space and then springs back ready for use with the minimum of effort.

The chair is available at all good furnishers and   **190**
department stores and we strongly urge you to try it
before reaching a decision. Only by sitting and reclining in
it will you really know just how extraordinarily comfortable
it is.

The Prescription Model Lamps are tax free and only   **191**
available against a medical certificate. The other two models
are subject to VAT, but are readily available from your local
electrical dealer. The nearest one to your home address is
——.

As you will gather from the enclosed material, there   **192**
are three ways in which you can treat your Western Red
Cedar weatherboarding. The first is the simplest and
consists of leaving it to weather naturally. Thousands of
Canadian and American householders do just this and in a
few years the wood takes on a silvery-grey colour which is
extremely attractive.

The second method is to attempt to preserve the
wood's original colour. This is not really to be recommended
unless the area to be treated is very small and the high
expense involved is considered worthwhile. We do not
recommend this solution because our tests indicate that it
takes a minimum of four coats of a good quality resinous
finish, careful sealing of the end grain and maintenance
every two or three years.

The third method lies somewhere between the other
two. It consists in applying a natural finish which
preserves the wood and encourages a more 'graceful' form
of weathering.

Which method you choose is very much a matter of
taste, but from the practical point of view, we recommend
the first or third procedures.

We recommend that you pay particular attention to   **193**
page 3, which gives instructions on nailing. Western Red
Cedar contains chemicals which cause staining when the
wood is in contact with ferrous metals. Weatherboarding
should therefore always be fixed with copper, aluminium or
sheradized nails.

194   The first rule you would do well to observe is to keep your blinds dusted, rather than letting dust accumulate and cake on them. You can do this quite simply with a duster or with one of the special brushes on the market.

As for actual washing, this is quite simple too. All you do is take down the blind and wash it in water containing a little detergent. Put an old sock or mitten on your hand and wash the slats. Rinse well and leave the blind to dry on its own before replacing it at the window.

195   The ____ cleaning tongs are specially made for the purpose and the enclosed leaflet explains just how simple it is to keep your Venetian blinds spotless with this handy and inexpensive little tool.

196   If you prefer to hand over the whole chore to someone else, why not use us? We have a very quick and efficient cleaning service. All you do is give us a ring and we come and collect your blinds, returning them to you in a matter of days sparkling clean and ready to go up again.

197   The enclosed folder will give you details of several tools especially designed for the purpose. You do not need them all, of course. It is simply a matter of selecting the one which appeals to you most.

The ____ brush, for instance, will help you dust your blinds down in a jiffy.

The ____ tongs dipped in warm water and detergent will clean even your greasy kitchen blind with no difficulty.

The ____ sprinkler brush is ideal for larger cleaning jobs. Get your blind out on the lawn. Attach your brush to your garden hose and clean your blind as you do your car.

It is true that your cooker will need to be dismounted **198**
to enable the connections to be fitted behind, but this is a
simple enough job and our fitter will be glad to carry it out
for you any time you like.

We have filled in the necessary details for you on the
enclosed order form and all you need to do to order your
spit is to sign your name at the bottom of the form. Your
spit will be delivered and fitted within two weeks of our
receiving the order.

The cost involved is £25 for the spit, plus £12 for **199**
fitting.

We can deliver the spit from stock.

The cost of the spit if £____, plus £____ for fitting. **200**

Unfortunately, however, we cannot promise to deliver
one to you in less than three months from date of receipt of
your order.

The spit has been so immensely popular that our
production line has fallen behind. We are quite sure,
however, that once you get your spit and discover what a
pleasure it is to cook with it, you will agree that the wait
was well worthwhile.

Closing paragraphs

The order was shipped by ____ on ____. **201**

Kindly collect from The XYZ Company Ltd of your **202**
city the full amount of our invoice, against the enclosed
documents.

Please collect the amount of the L/C from Soc. An. **203**
Mario Bianchi, against surrender of the enclosed
documents.

204   Please deliver the enclosed documents to Joseph Doakes PLC upon payment of the invoice amount in full.

205   We look forward with interest to your further news.

206   If you need any further help from us, do please let us know.

207   I look forward to hearing from you soon.

208   We hope you will be in touch with us soon.

209   We certainly hope you will let us quote you on your next ____ job.

210   Why not put us to the test at the next opportunity?

211   Because we sell the ____ direct to the consuming public, we are able to offer it to you at the very low price of £____. An order form is enclosed, as well as a return envelope.

We look forward to receiving your order soon.

212   Don't forget – try the ____ soon.

213   If there is any further information you would like to have, do please let us know.

214   We hope you will soon be enjoying all the benefits which the ____ sun lamps can give you.

215   We hope that this letter and the enclosures satisfactorily answer all your questions. If not, do let us know and we will do our best to help you further.

All of the tools are on sale at most hardware stores, but should you have any difficulty finding them, please let us know. **216**

All these handy tools are available direct from us. If you will just complete the enclosed order form, ticking the items required, we shall be happy to send them to you by return. **217**

For your convenience, we are enclosing a list of stockists in your area. **218**

If you prefer, you can of course order the spit from your local Electricity Board. The choice is yours. **219**

We look forward to hearing from you further. **220**

We can ship at once. May we fill your order? **221**

6

Credit and Collection

As we move relentlessly towards a cashless society it becomes ever easier to spend our money and, by a strange paradox, harder to recuperate moneys due us. For some time it has been possible to go to a restaurant, have lunch, enjoy a shopping expedition then return home without needing a single penny in cash. In the UK, goods can be ordered by Prestel without stepping outside the front door and credit cards proliferate.

Banks, which were the first to issue credit cards, have already discovered to their cost that it is far easier to issue one than it is to get payment from some card holders. Even ordinary businesses, whose only brush with credit granting is the almost proverbial '30 days net', are finding it takes longer to get paid.

This being the case, it follows that a more dynamic and scientific collection method needs to be used. Sticking humorous labels to past-due accounts does sometimes work, but this hardly constitutes a complete and well-thought out strategy.

A series of well-written collection letters, sent out at intervals of ten to fifteen days, is a better plan.

The most important point to bear in mind is that a collection letter is in every sense a sales letter. Instead of selling the customer your goods, you are selling him on sending you the money he owes you and you want to achieve this without losing his goodwill. If you think of it in this way, everything else will fall naturally into place.

You will, for instance, bear in mind that you are competing for his money with several other companies, for people seldom owe money to one company alone. Your letter will aim to persuade him to pay *your* bill rather than the other half dozen in his 'In-tray'. How, then, are you going to persuade him? Certainly not by antagonizing him. Any lawyer will tell you that you simply cannot antagonize a person and influence him in your favour at the same time.

You will be more likely to influence him favourably if you put yourself in his shoes and try to see the problem from *his* point of view; if you use the 'you' approach; if you write him a human, understanding letter, rather than the curt, indifferent, ice-cold missives which so often go out.

Your collection letters should follow the same pattern as your sales letters in that they should have an attention-getting opening and an unequivocal close.

78

Just as any salesperson worth his salt does not hesitate to ask for the order, so your letter must end in asking for the money or for whatever move you want your correspondent to make.

Collection letters should not be written at random, but should follow a steady progression. They should be a series in five stages:

1 *First reminders*. These should go out to all overdue accounts as first, second and even third reminders, as well as to those customers who have made further purchases without settling their outstanding accounts.

2 *Follow-ups*. If your first reminders have done no good, then you will follow up by reminding the customer of your trade terms, asking whether he needs copies of invoices, pointing out that he is jeopardizing his credit standing, and intimating that his credit will be cut if he does not meet his obligations. You will not, of course, use all these points in the same letter, but use the theme with variations in several letters.

3 *Change of tactics*. If you have had no luck by now, you are faced with a difficult case. You will need to try a change of pace and you can afford to try something really unorthodox, since you have little to lose. You might try the humorous approach, for instance. It frequently works where all else fails, and what have you to lose at this stage?

4 *Acknowledgment of payments on account*. This stage can be reached at any time and not necessarily after No. 3. If a customer sends you a small cheque on account, you will need to ask for the balance, but this does not mean you should be ungracious and omit to thank him for the amount received.

5 *The last resort*. If all these measures fail, there is nothing for it but to turn over the account for collection. If you advise the customer beforehand that you intend to do this, nine times out of ten he will pay up without further ado. Never do it until you have tried everything else and, above all, never threaten to do it if you don't mean it. It is a very serious step to take, a point of no return in fact, and on no account should it be used as a bluff.

In the USA, where they have been selling on credit for longer than in Britain, fashions in collection techniques change almost as frequently as fashions in dress. Some years ago it was all the rage to send out printed cards as reminders and they were found sufficient to bring in payment in 75 to 85 percent of all cases. It seems a method well worth trying.

Have three or four sets to a series, so they do not become an old familiar story to habitual slow payers. For the same reason, change the whole series once a year.

Not only have the cards been found to work, but they have three additional advantages over other types of reminder:

1 A series of cards makes it extremely easy for you to follow up overdue accounts regularly and, as you know, regularity of follow-up is one of the cardinal rules of collection strategy.

2 Printed cards are much cheaper to produce than an individually typed letter and far more effective than those execrable form-letters which some

companies still send out. The cards can go out both to companies who owe you money and to retail customers. An attractive card in a pastel shade with a matching envelope is very suitable for retail customers. Cards addressed to the latter should be couched in informal terms and should be free from accounting jargon, which not everyone understands.

3 The printed card has the psychological advantage of being impersonal enough not to make the slow payer feel he or she is being singled out as such. The recipient knows it is a card which thousands of people get and consequently it does not make him or her feel guilty and therefore antagonistic to the sender.

The suggestions for printed cards which follow are not separated into isolated paragraphs, since this is neither practical nor useful in this case. Some of them are reprinted by kind permission of a world-famous American corporation which prefers to remain anonymous. A few years ago this same company used to send out cheerful cartoons as first reminders and two of them are shown in Figures 8 and 9.

The follow-up letters given later in this chapter can, of course, be keyboarded in advance, stored into your wordprocessor's memory in a well-ordered series, and retrieved as needed. Names, addresses and such details as amount outstanding, can then be matched in to perfection, resulting, to all intents and purposes, in an individually typed letter.

Reminder cards

222   YOU HAVE SUCH AN EXCELLENT RECORD . . .
that if, for once, you fail to pay your invoices when due we know something has gone wrong.
Perhaps our last statement didn't reach you, or our figures do not agree with yours. In either case, won't you please let us hear from you right away?

CREDIT DEPARTMENT

223   MAY WE REMIND YOU
that there's a balance due on your account? This may have escaped your attention so perhaps, if you have not just done so, you'd be good enough to put a cheque in the post to us right away. If you have already taken care of it, please accept our sincere thanks.

Amount due: £____

If It's in the Mail . . .

we mean a check for the overdue balance of
please accept our sincere "Thank You".

But if you haven't sent us a payment, won't you kindly put one in the mail today.

Cordially,

Figure 8 and Figure 9   Two examples of a world-famous American corporation's method of asking for payment

You'd Be Surprised . . .

how often we send a customer a reminder
about an overdue account only to receive
a check in the very next mail.

So if that should happen in this case, please excuse this card and accept our sincere
"Thanks". But if you haven't sent payment for the balance of   won't
you please do so right away.

Cordially,

224   WE KNOW HOW DIFFICULT IT IS . . .
to go over every invoice and make out a cheque for it
promptly every month. But your balance is now a little
overdue and we would like you to send us a cheque as soon
as possible.
Of course if you have just sent us a remittance, please
excuse this reminder and accept our sincere thanks.

Amount due: £____

225   LOST IN THE MAIL?
We mean our recent reminder that your unpaid balance is
now long overdue. We realise you are not purposely
withholding payment, but would greatly appreciate your
putting a cheque in the post to us today.

Amount due: £____

226   SINCE WE'RE NEVER SURE . . .
whether our reminders reach the right person, we are
sending you this second one about your balance as shown
below.
So if you haven't sent us a cheque yet, won't you please
make every effort to get one off right away? Thank you for
your prompt co-operation.

Amount: £____

227   YOU PROBABLY INTENDED . . .
to send us the cheque we wrote to you about. But it has
apparently escaped your attention, since we haven't
received it yet.
Of course, if it's on its way – many thanks. But if not, won't
you please put your remittance for the amount shown
below in the post right away? Your prompt co-operation
will be sincerely appreciated.

Amount: £____

DO YOU RECALL . . .   **228**
our sending you a reminder a short time ago about your
balance as shown below, which is now overdue? If it went
astray, won't you kindly check right away to see what is
causing the delay? Then get a payment off to us within the
next day or two.
Of course if you have just sent us a remittance, please
excuse this card and accept our thanks.

Amount due: £____

DIDN'T YOU RECEIVE . . .   **229**
the reminder we sent you recently about your overdue
balance, as shown below?
If you have just sent us a payment, please accept our
sincere thanks. Otherwise, won't you make a special effort
to get a cheque off to us right away?
Thank you.

Amount: £____

IT WON'T TAKE LONG . . .   **230**
to check and see why a payment hasn't been sent for your
overdue balance about which we reminded you. So will you
please take a minute right now to find out what is causing
the delay? Then put a cheque in the post within the next
day or two, if you have not already done so.
Your prompt co-operation will be appreciated.

Amount due £____

DID IT ESCAPE YOUR ATTENTION?   **231**
We mean that little reminder we sent you a short time ago
about your past due account.
If it did, won't you please check and see why a payment has
not been sent to us? Then make a special effort to get a
remittance off without delay, if you have not already done
so.
Thank you for your prompt co-operation.

Amount: £____

232   DID YOU REALIZE ...
that an additional amount has matured since we reminded
you that your balance was overdue? Obviously you didn't,
otherwise you most certainly would have sent us a cheque.
So won't you please do so right away before it slips your
mind again?

Amount due: £___

233   YOU'D PROBABLY FEEL ...
we were negligent if we didn't remind you that an
additional amount has matured since our last reminder that
your account is overdue.
If you have any questions about these unpaid invoices,
please let us know at once. But if your records agree with
ours, won't you please send us your cheque now, unless of
course it is already on the way.

Total now overdue: £___

234   YOU UNDOUBTEDLY WANT US ...
to keep you fully informed about the condition of your
account. That's why we're reminding you that another
amount has matured since our recent notice.
So if you haven't already taken care of this outstanding
balance, please let us have your cheque right away. You
may be sure your prompt attention will be sincerely
appreciated.

Total now overdue: £___

235   IT'S GROWING LIKE TOPSY ...
We mean that overdue balance we have reminded you about
so many times. Additional amounts have fallen due and
each new amount makes it harder for you to catch up. We
would not like this to become a real problem for you and
urge you to put a cheque in the mail to us right away.
Otherwise, please at least let us know when we can expect
it.
We are counting on your prompt co-operation.

Amount now due: £___

Follow-up letters

Some of the letters which follow can be used instead of the cards if you prefer the more formal approach of a letter.

Opening paragraphs

Dear Sirs,   **236**

>   You will understand, we are sure, why we remind customers about their overdue balances. You probably do so, too.

Dear Sirs,   **237**

>   You undoubtedly do it, too – that is remind your customers when they fall a little behind in their payments.

Dear Sirs,   **238**

>   Time flies so fast that perhaps you didn't realize your account shows an overdue balance of £____.

Dear Sirs,   **239**

>   Since our recent reminders about your account, there has been a change in the amount due.

Dear Sirs,   **240**

>   Several reminders have been sent to you about your overdue balance, but your cheque still hasn't arrived.

Dear Sirs,   **241**

>   You probably don't mean to keep us in the dark, but you are.

242   Dear Sirs,

   Your overdue balance is getting quite old. Although we've sent several reminders, no payment or explanation has been received.

243   Dear Mr Green,

   Perhaps you did not realize that the balance on the attached statement is long overdue.

244   Dear Sirs,

   It's difficult to understand why you haven't paid your overdue account totalling £____.

245   Dear Mrs Whitman,

   We very much regret to have to inconvenience you, but since you have not replied to our previous letters about your long overdue account, we have no alternative but to discontinue your charge privileges.

246   Dear Mr Biggs,

   Don't you agree that it is better to discuss a problem in person rather than attempting to solve it by mail? Why, then, don't you come in and see me about your account?

247   Dear Sirs,

   Thank you for your cheque for the sum of £____. While we greatly appreciate this partial payment, we must remind you that your account still shows an overdue balance of £____.

248   Dear Sirs,

   We have tried to avoid it, but since you have not replied to our many reminders, we have no alternative but to turn over your account to our solicitors for collection.

Dear Mr Brown,   **249**

Many concerns, we know, only pay promptly those
companies whose products they need most. This may seem
like a good idea, yet it is a fallacy, for a good credit standing
is not based on how well you pay <u>some</u> of your suppliers,
but all of them. Furthermore, poor payers soon get known
and creditors who are discriminated against may demand
immediate payment. Where would you be then?

Dear Sirs,   **250**

Have you ever stopped to consider how inconvenient
it would be if we were to take legal action to collect the
balance of your long overdue account? First of all there
would be the embarrasment and expenses involved and
secondly it would affect your credit standing, which is an
asset we are sure you do not undervalue.

Dear Ms Redman,   **251**

Many thanks for your cheque in the amount of
£____. This leaves only the following invoices still
outstanding:

> Invoice No. .... in the amount of £____
>   "   " ...   "   "   "   " £____
>   "   " ...   "   "   "   " £____

Dear Sirs,   **252**

We certainly appreciate receiving your cheque for
£____. We are wondering, however, whether you realize that
the following invoices are still outstanding:

> Invoice No. .... amounting to £____
>   "   " ...   "   " £____

253   Dear Sirs,

We feel sure you would agree with us that it would be a shame to terminate a relationship which has been so pleasant. But the amount you owe us is now long overdue and unless we hear from you by return you leave us no alternative but to turn your account over to our solicitors.

The body of the letter

254   So if you haven't already sent us a cheque for £____, will you please send us one within the next few days?

255   You will therefore understand why we are writing to you today to ask you to send us a cheque for £____ to cover your overdue balance.

256   Won't you please therefore send us a cheque within the next few days and clear this matter up?

257   If you haven't already done so, won't you please take a moment now to send us a cheque or let us know when we may expect it?

258   If you have some questions or need more information, please let us know promptly. We will help you immediately.

259   We've sent you several reminders about your overdue account, but have not received payment or heard from you. So you can realize why we're puzzled.

260   Won't you take a few minutes to let us hear from you if there is any query? Or, if your records agree with ours, why not send us a cheque for as much as you can spare and tell us when the balance will follow?

Your account is seriously overdue, so it is important **261**
that you take immediate action. Unless a cheque has just
been sent, please post one without delay.

Unfortunately, you leave us no choice but to withhold **262**
deliveries until this amount is paid. However, if you will
send us a cheque for £___ right away we shall be happy to
resume shipping your orders without further delay.

Could it be that your records do not agree with ours **263**
and that you have a question with regard to one of the
invoices?

Is the amount shown below correct? Or is there a **264**
credit due to you to be deducted from it? If such is the case,
or if you have any other query with regard to this long
overdue account, please let us know right away.

If on the other hand, the amount shown is correct,
then won't you please let us have your cheque without
further delay?

We are sorry indeed to have to do this, since we **265**
know what a convenience your charge account has been to
you.

Why not keep your credit standing and the
convenience of your Wellby account by sending us a cheque
right away? If this is impossible at the moment, then why
not come in and discuss with us a way to pay off your old
bills in easy instalments?

I know that at times it is difficult to clear up an old **266**
account and I really am most anxious to co-operate with
you in every way I can.

Do please come in as soon as possible, or, if you
prefer, why not phone me at _____ and we can discuss it
then?

267   We do not write to you as we do with any wish to cause you hardship. On the contrary, we are most anxious to co-operate with you and find a way for you to pay off this long-overdue account. In fact, if you send us a cheque for £____ right away, together with a plan for paying off the balance in several instalments, we shall be happy to accommodate you.

268   If you are having difficulty in sending us a cheque for the whole amount, why not sit down right now and write us a cheque for £____ on account? Then do the same thing on the first day of the next three months and by then the whole miserable business will have vanished into thin air! It really is as simple as that.

269   Yet we are not demanding that you send us a cheque for the whole amount right away. All we ask is that you send us £____ on account and let us know when to expect the balance, in one or two instalments if you wish.

270   You surely realize how unpleasant and costly it is to let a matter like this go to court. But this is not all, of course. It would also adversely affect your credit standing and consequently your reputation as a company.

     This is why we have waited so long before taking this very serious step.

271   Why not save yourself from this needless embarrassment and expense by sending us a cheque for the amount given below right away?

272   If you have any queries on any of the outstanding invoices, please let us know at once. Otherwise, we would greatly appreciate your passing them for payment as soon as possible.

Since both of them are long overdue, we would   **273**
appreciate your early settlement to bring your account
completely up to date. Of course, should you have a query on
either of them or if your records differ from ours, please let
us know right away.

Since this has been outstanding for such a long time,   **274**
we feel we must ask you to let us know when we can expect
your cheque to bring your account completely up to date.

Closing paragraphs

Your prompt co-operation will be greatly appreciated.   **275**

Of course, if you have just sent payment, please   **276**
excuse this untimely reminder and accept our sincere
thanks.

Thank you for your prompt co-operation.   **277**

However, if the account is correct, please send us   **278**
your remittance right away. We are counting on you to act
promptly.

PS   This is what is overdue: £____

This is urgent, so please send us your cheque now or   **279**
let us know right away what is holding it up. We are
counting on your prompt action.

PS   The overdue balance is: £____

We'll be glad to co-operate with you in bringing your   **280**
account up to date in this way. Please get in touch with us
by return of post.

PS   The overdue balance is: £____

281   If such is the case, please let us know by return. Otherwise, please let us have your remittance without delay.

282   Your prompt co-operation will be greatly appreciated.

Amount due: £____

283   We count on your prompt action.

284   I look forward to hearing from you.

285   As we are anxious to give you quick and efficient service all the time, we'd greatly appreciate hearing from you right away.

286   We'll be looking forward to receiving the first instalment within the next two or three days.

287   Could anything be fairer? Surely not. Do then sit down right away and write out a cheque for £____. You will be surprised at how quickly this long overdue account can be cleared up.

We shall be looking out for your cheque!

288   Why not remove the risk altogether by sending us your cheque for £____ right away?

289   We can wait no longer, however, and <u>must</u> have your cheque in our hands within ten days.

Amount due: £____

290   We are anxious to make things easy for you, and we hope you will accept this sensible suggestion. Let us hear from you soon.

Refusing and restricting credit

As with many other things, prevention is better than cure in the case of bad debts. There are many instances when it would be wiser to refuse credit outright, others where it would pay you to restrict it to a certain figure, and cases where past experience advises you to alter a customer's terms of payment.

The letters which follow cover various cases of this kind, both in the retail and in the wholesale field.

Opening paragraphs

Dear Ms Wheeler,   **291**

We were very glad to receive your letter asking us to open a charge account in your name. This expression of your confidence in and appreciation of our store means a lot to us.

Dear Ms Jenkins,   **292**

Thank you for your letter requesting a Seldon's charge account. It is an expression of confidence and goodwill that we greatly appreciate.

Dear Miss Constable,   **293**

Thank you for your letter of May 21, requesting a charge account with our department store.

Dear Mr Brown,   **294**
Your Order No. 875
Your initial order is almost ready for shipment, but, much as we would like to do so, we are unable to ship it to you on credit on the basis of the information you sent us.

Dear Ms Weston,   **295**

There is nothing we would like better than to issue you with a Bloggs Credit Card, as you request.

296   Dear Mr Green,

   We very much appreciate your interest in the Tiger range of products and would very much like to welcome you as our Agent for the West Country.

297   Dear Ms Ball,

   We are sure you realize how much we appreciate the steady stream of orders you have been sending us for a number of months. However, it will not have escaped your attention that we are constantly obliged to remind you that the cheques you send us from time to time come nowhere near to keeping your account up to date. In fact, in spite of your periodical cheques, your account oustanding grows steadily larger.

The body of the letter

298   Perhaps at some later date we shall be in a position to comply with your request; in the meantime we very much hope you will visit the store often and enjoy the high fashion, courteous service, and fair prices which it offers.

299   As you know, when such a request is received a routine credit investigation is usually carried out and a decision made in each individual case. Unfortunately our information in support of your application is incomplete and we would therefore appreciate your calling at the Credit Department to clear up one or two points.

300   While we are not at the moment in a position to comply with your request, we hope it will be possible to do so later on.

301   Perhaps there is some other information you can send us; meanwhile, to save time, it might be a good plan for you to authorize us to ship this initial order COD.

Unfortunately, however, we are informed that you   **302**
tend to be rather slow in paying invoices and we feel that
perhaps you would have difficulty in meeting our terms,
which are 2 per cent 10 days, 30 days net. This may very
well be a temporary situation, however, and we would be
more than glad to reconsider the matter later on.

We are sure you will appreciate that we cannot go on   **303**
indefinitely doing business with you on such an
unprofitable basis and we would therefore like to suggest
different terms for future orders. We propose that we ship
your future orders COD, at least until such time as your
outstanding invoices have been paid.

Once the slate has been wiped clean perhaps we can
think of another basis on which to do business which will
prove satisfactory to both companies.

However, like all other companies extending credit,   **304**
we have to make sure a person is able to meet our terms,
which are 30 days net. It appears from information
gathered that you usually need a little longer. We may well
have been misinformed, however, and if you will kindly let
us have the names and addresses of two companies with
whom you have established credit, we shall be delighted to
consider your application further.

Closing paragraphs

We look forward to meeting you.   **305**

We look forward to welcoming you in the store as   **306**
usual and assure you of our desire to serve you to the best
of our ability always.

We look forward to hearing from you promptly and   **307**
will hold your order pending your instructions.

308   We are very reluctant to have to write to you in this vein, but feel sure that, as a business person, you will understand our position.

309   We are sorry we are unable to be of service to you in this instance and sincerely hope that conditions will soon improve for you.

7

Adjustments and Complaints

Your customer's goodwill should be your most precious possession, for without it you will not remain in business for long. 'Goodwill', in fact, becomes a very tangible asset when a business is sold, as everyone knows. Unfortunately, however, business people all too frequently forget this fact and treat customers almost as if they were enemies. The policy of 'let the buyer beware' is still all too prevalent, alas. Such a policy is that of the itinerant pedlar, who sells his shoddy wares to whoever is prepared to buy them, secure in the knowledge that, by the morrow, he will have moved on, perhaps never to return. Why should he worry if the customer is displeased with his purchase? He will probably never need to sell him anything again.

The serious manufacturer, wholesaler or retailer, on the other hand, hopes to be in business not merely next week, but next year, ten years hence and probably well beyond that. He therefore needs to sell each customer not only one article, but a great many of them, perhaps for the customer's lifetime. He wants his customer to recommend his goods to his relatives and friends. In short, he wants his goodwill.

It follows, therefore, that you simply cannot afford to sell a customer an item and then wash your hands of him. It should be important to you that your customer is satisfied with his purchase. If he is not and writes to tell you so, your first concern should be to give him satisfaction, to leave him thinking well of your company, even if not of your product.

This simple fact is thoroughly understood in the USA, where any retailer will take back a purchase which has proved unsatisfactory and a manufacturer, approached direct about one of his products, will practically turn somersaults to keep a single customer in the fold. In Britain one company stands out like a beacon for its excellent policy on customer relations. It is Marks and Spencer PLC. As you know, if you buy something from M & S and are dissatisfied for any reason at all, all you need to do is return it and it will be exchanged or your money refunded without question. As Marcus Sieff once explained in the House of Lords, the company's customer-returns policy serves not only to keep customers satisfied but also as a last check on quality.

One can feel quite confident that any customer writing a letter of complaint to M & S receives a prompt, friendly, and satisfying reply.

The first thing to bear in mind when answering a letter of complaint is that your reply should aim not to prove the customer wrong, but to give him satisfaction. Your reply should be prompt, friendly and sincere. It should be written from the customer's point of view and show a real desire to solve his problem.

If your product is at fault, admit it quite frankly. Nothing irritates a customer more than excuses and attempts to turn the argument in your favour. If she has used your shampoo and it has made her fair fall out, she is not interested in your assurances that it is a high-grade product and has been thoroughly tested.

A customer is sometimes quite angry and will write an emotional letter which does not contain the facts you need to investigate his complaint properly. In such cases you must get the facts from him and do it without irritating him still further. On the other hand, give *him* the facts in turn, but do so diplomatically. Do not appear to be telling him what to do, or to be implying that he doesn't know how to use your product correctly.

Do not attempt to win an argument and never humiliate a customer, even if he *is* in the wrong. Remember the sales representative who won the argument but lost the sale. It can be just the same with a dissatisfied customer. In fact, a permanently dissatisfied customer can do you untold harm. He will not keep his dissatisfaction to himself. He will spread it around, tell his friends, relatives, and colleagues. Your business cannot afford even one dissatisfied customer. So let your letters to him aim at pleasing him and bringing him back into the fold.

All the letters which follow are based on this philosophy. If your company still believes in *caveat emptor*, then your most urgent need is for a new set of sales policies.

Opening paragraphs

310   Dear Mr King,

Your anger upon receiving a second shipment of damaged filters is most understandable and we hasten to assure you that we are every bit as distressed as you are at this unfortunate occurrence.

311   Dear Ms Allan,

We quite understand your losing patience over the seemingly endless flood of trouble which has accompanied our processing of your last order. We, too, in your shoes, would be just as angry. Perhaps, though, you can imagine how very distressing this is for us too, knowing as you do how highly we value good customers such as yourself.

Dear Mr Wallace,   **312**

     We are sending off to you today a shipment of galvanized steel rails to replace the ones about which you wrote us in your letter of September 23.

Dear Miss Miles,   **313**

     We thank you for writing to us about the dress which is not giving you satisfaction, as we are most anxious to see that all our customers are pleased with the purchases they make at ____'s.

Dear Jack,   **314**

     It's always a pleasure to hear from you, even though some of your letters, such as that of February 25, do not bring good news.

Dear Ms Klein,   **315**

     To err is human and, unfortunately, we appear to have been all too human in this particular instance. All we can do now is make honourable amends and this we are only too anxious to do.

Dear Mr Good,   **316**

     I'm afraid I have no explanation to offer for the irritating mistakes which have been dogging us every inch of the way in the filling of your last order. As you know, this is not typical of our service and I offer this comment not as an excuse, for there is no excuse for under-par service, but simply as a reminder that we normally do better and one of our foremost aims is to please our customers.

Dear Mr Gamage,   **317**

     We are very sorry to hear from your letter of April 22 that your first experience with your new ____ cine camera proved so disappointing.

318   Dear Mrs Green,

Thank you for bringing to our attention the unfortunate experience you had with the ____ Foodmixer, as this gives us the opportunity to help you.

319   Dear Miss Mathews,

We were very sorry to learn of your disappointment in the ____ Shampoo, the greater no doubt because you were naturally looking forward to the excellent results you had every right to expect.

320   Dear Ms Rhodes,

We were very sorry to learn from your letter of April 5 the deplorable condition in which your last order of glass reached you and hasten to assure you that we are only too anxious to adjust this unfortunate matter in the way most satisfactory to you.

321   Dear Sirs,

We have your letter of January 6 from which it appears that your records and ours do not agree as to the amount still outstanding in your account.

322   Dear Mrs Gilmore,

Thank you for bringing to our attention the trouble you experienced in getting the service you have every right to expect from our coats and suits department.

323   Dear Miss Miller,

We were most distressed to hear of your experience with the silk blouse which you returned to us for inspection.

Dear Mr French,   **324**

     We were very sorry to learn from your letter of June
4 that our shipment of worsted rags was two bales short.

Dear Mr Green,   **325**

     It was good of you to take the time to write to us
about your experience with our ___ 'Italian by Ear' records,
since this give us the opportunity of explaining how best
you can benefit from this unique course.

Dear Mr Smith,   **326**

     We were surprised and disappointed to learn that our
shipment of oil filters has still not reached you.

Dear Mrs Jones,   **327**

     We were very distressed to learn that Mr Seymour's
visit proved so inconvenient and unwelcome and hasten to
assure you that this was not at all our intention when we
asked him to call on you regarding our line of ___ in which
you had expressed an interest.

Dear Ms Stewart,   **328**

     We are sorry to hear that we made an error in filling
your Order No. 0065.

Dear Mr Fleming,   **329**

     We have your letter of April 15 in which you tell us
that you are not in agreement with our invoice No. 00765
dated April 10 covering our recent shipment of ___.

Dear Ms Fisher,   **330**

     I certainly cannot deny that the estimate I sent you
goes well beyond the figure you mentioned as being your
'ceiling'.

The body of the letter

331   You will be pleased to learn that a fresh supply of filters is already on its way to you and should reach you within a day or two.

332   At the same time we have instructed our local representative, Ms Jones, to call on you as soon as possible and examine the packing and the filters in an effort to ascertain how this unfortunate coincidence could have happened.

333   We are still investigating this matter on our shop floor in an endeavour to find out just what happened and how it can be avoided in future.

334   We do believe that the whole matter is now about to be settled to your complete satisfaction. The remaining missing pieces have been sent to you today by air parcel post, so that by tomorrow or the day after the complete order should be in your hands.

335   We have investigated this matter and find that, just as you had surmised, an unsatisfactory roll of steel strip had somehow been used and the resulting rails had failed to be caught by our quality control net.

336   We really cannot explain how the rails could have rusted and are most grateful to you for bringing this unfortunate matter to our attention. You can be assured that we shall take it up with our supplier; meanwhile, a new shipment is on its way to you.

It is our policy to refund the purchase price of a **337**
garment which is returned to us in good condition within
five days of purchase, if the customer is dissatisfied with it
for any reason.

If you will therefore bring the dress in, we shall be
happy to exchange it for another one or refund the
purchase price to you in full.

We were very distressed to hear about all the **338**
complaints you have had on our Model KW-52 ____.
Unfortunately, we have had similar complaints from other
areas and our development department is now investigating
what appears to be a fault in the ____.

Please apologize to your customers on our behalf and
send them a replacement. We have already withdrawn the
KW-52 from circulation pending the result of our
investigation.

We further suggest that you hold on to any **339**
remaining stocks of this new model until the fault has been
corrected. Our accounts department will be sending you a
credit note for the whole shipment and, later on, when the
fault has been located and corrected, we will arrange to
replace your remaining stock with perfect units.

To help you to secure the kind of results you hoped **340**
for when purchasing our ____ camera, we are enclosing a
booklet called 'Home Films Made Easy'. It was especially
prepared for our customers by our technical department
and we are sure you will find it most useful.

It is rather difficult for us to decide just what went **341**
wrong without having a few more facts to work upon.
Would you therefore be good enough to answer the
questions on the attached sheet? This should enable us to
locate the source of the trouble and help you to secure
better results next time.

342   We have, in fact, already sent off to you a complete set of ____, in the right colour and size this time, and will be obliged if you will kindly return your present set to us.

343   I do hope that, in spite of the delays, errors and confusions, you are now quite satisfied with your ____. If there is anything at all we can do to make up for the inconvenience you have been caused, do please let us know.

344   You will notice a tiny lever on the side of the Mixer. It can be set at any one of the three positions marked 1, 2, and 3. Each of these positions is suitable for a particular kind of mix, whether it be just plain eggs or a heavy cake mix. In time, it becomes quite simple to remember to set the lever on '1' for eggs and '3' for heavy cake mixes, but until you have got used to this, it is best to look it up in the instructions book which went with the beater. You will find this information on page 2.

As for your <u>roux</u>, this does sometimes curdle, for one of several reasons. The milk may have been too cold or there was not enough flour as opposed to butter in the mixture. There is a very easy remedy for this situation, however. Simply add a few drops of cold water to your <u>roux</u> and continue beating until it re-amalgamates. Then continue adding your milk. For making <u>roux</u>, the lever on your ____ Foodmixer should be set at '2', as it says in the instruction booklet.

345   It does happen, however, that some people's skins are unduly sensitive and such people are unfortunately unable to use ____ Shampoo to good advantage.

This is the reason why the instruction leaflet recommends rubbing a tiny squeeze of the shampoo into the inside of your elbow before proceeding with the job. If after about eight hours your skin shows the slightest tendency to redness, you should not use the shampoo.

346   Please let us know whether you want us to forward the two missing bales on their own, or whether you prefer that we add them to your next shipment.

We are therefore enclosing a complete tabulation of all our invoices from January 2 1985 to date, as well as all your payments. This will show you why we believe the balance still outstanding to be £____.   **347**

We have investigated this matter and it appears that the assistant who served you was a relatively new girl, and therefore not yet fully trained in the standards of service we believe in.   **348**

We have spoken to the assistant concerned and you may be assured that your unfortunate experience in the coats and suits department will not be repeated.

Unfortunately, yours is not the first complaint we have had about these blouses and we have taken the matter up with the manufacturer. The error is apparently his and the blouses should not have been marked 'Hand Washable'. They should, rather, be dry-cleaned only.   **349**

We have investigated this matter with our packing department and it does appear that the glass was packed in our usual thorough way. No reason for the breakage has come to light at this end. We can only conclude that it was subject to exceptionally rough handling en route.   **350**

The important point, however, is for you to get your complete order as quickly as possible and we have today made a duplicate shipment replacing all the pieces which arrived broken.

351   First of all you should listen to the record straight through, without attempting to understand what is being said. This exercise 'educates the ear' to the sound of the Italian language.

Then read the lesson in the book, listen to the record once again and repeat the sentences after the speaker. You will then know exactly what both questions and answers mean. Repeat this exercise several times and then listen to the questions only and give the answers yourself, checking afterwards to see if you were right.

You can then read the questions from the book, write down the answers and check back with the book or the record.

By alternating in this way over and over again, you will eventually become thoroughly familiar with the questions and know exactly how to answer them in perfect Italian.

352   We have been in touch with our shippers and they insist that this particular parcel should have reached you several days ago.

Pending further investigations, we are sending you a fresh supply by air freight in order that you may not be inconvenienced further.

353   Since our line of ____ is such an extensive one and can be tailored so closely to a customer's actual needs, we find that a visit by our sales representative helps the customer decide just which pieces fit her particular requirements best.

Our representative's intention is certainly not to put any pressure on the customer to buy, but simply and solely to put his knowledge of our products and of customers' needs at your disposal in making such an important decision.

If you will kindly return the wrong lengths to us we   **354**
will immediately replace them with the correct ones.
Alternatively, to save time, if you will let us know how
many incorrect lengths the shipment contained, we will
send off a new shipment right away.

We really cannot understand why this should be so,   **355**
since the prices invoiced are those given in our latest price
list, dated January 6 1985, which is certainly in your
hands.

Your complaint is therefore fully justified and no   **356**
doubt I deserved the rap on the knuckles which you gave
me. Prices do rise very quickly, however, and what fits
within a budget today goes slightly over it tomorrow. If you
multiply this unfortunate phenomenon by one hundred or
more, you will appreciate how easy it is to find yourself
quoting a client way beyond his 'ceiling'.

Fortunately there is a remedy, albeit a somewhat
disappointing one; it involves cutting out some of the
luxuries we had contemplated. Offhand, I can think of three:
the double-glazed windows, the built-in vacuumation, and
the terrazzo floors in kitchen, bathroom and toilets.

The prices you mention are from our old price list   **357**
which was replaced with a new one on January 6 of this
year. A copy of this up-to-date price list is enclosed, but you
certainly should have had one, since we sent it to all our
customers several months back.

Closing paragraphs

We look forward to hearing from you again giving us   **358**
the details we need in order to help you.

We are very sorry about your dissatisfaction with our   **359**
____ and greatly appreciate the friendly manner in which
you brought this problem to our attention and so enabled us
to put it right.

360   We sincerely hope that the adjustment we suggest will merit your approval and we look forward to hearing from you further.

361   I think both you and your customer have been exceptionally patient over this unfortunate occurrence. Do please convey this message to him, together with our thanks for his co-operation.

362   We are sorry indeed you were dissatisfied with the dress and look forward to putting the matter right when you call at the store.

363   I am working out a new estimate based on these suggestions and will let you have it within the next few days. Meanwhile, if you can think of any other items you feel you could live without, perhaps you would let me know, as this would help to whittle down the price even further.

364   We look forward to hearing from you further.

365   We hope this information clears up the misunderstanding and look forward to hearing from you.

366   We sincerely hope you will have nothing but successes in the future and appreciate this opportunity of being of service to you.

367   Should it turn out that you have one of those extremely sensitive skins, then we suggest you try our ____ Shampoo, especially developed for such cases. The enclosed leaflet will give you full details.

     We very much regret the inconvenience you have been caused and hope that the box of ____ products we are sending you will make up for it in some measure.

We greatly appreciate your bringing this matter to our attention, since it is only through the vigilance of good customers such as yourself that we are able to keep our service up to the high standards upon which we pride ourselves. **368**

If, therefore, you will return the blouse to the store, we shall be happy to replace it for you. **369**
We sincerely apologize for the inconvenience this has caused you and thank you for your patience and co-operation.

We wish you many happy hours <u>parlando italiano.</u> **370**

We do hope this explanation will make you feel happier about our representative's visit. **371**

Meanwhile, please accept our sincere apologies for this unprecedented occurrence and our grateful thanks for the patient and forbearing way in which you brought the matter to our attention. **372**

We very much regret the inconvenience you have experienced and hope you will now enjoy many years of trouble-free service from your ____. **373**

We sincerely regret the inconvenience you have suffered and thank you for bringing the matter to our attention. It is only when customers report such incidents that we are able to correct them. Thank you again for writing. **374**

In thanking you for bringing this matter to our attention, we should like to add our very best wishes for a happy and prosperous New Year. **375**

Thank you for writing and please accept our very best Christmas wishes. **376**

Making complaints

Inevitably, the day will come when you yourself have cause for complaint: a supplier has fallen down on a promise, you get a short shipment, goods arrive damaged, a product is not up to scratch – any of these situations may require a letter. As a member of the consuming public you no doubt also occasionally have cause for complaint. Poor service, shoddy merchandise, rudeness, badly prepared meals in hotel or restaurant, all call for comment and complaint to the appropriate quarters, either face to face or in writing.

Certainly, hotels and restaurants have improved considerably over the past few years. Similarly, the consumer protection movement has helped to shield the buying public from the worst excesses. Yet on the other hand, almost to prove that progress is *not* inevitable after all, the 'cowboy' operator has insinuated himself on the scene with his shoddy workmanship, broken promises and sky-high prices. He too is being brought under control, but meanwhile it is up to consumers to stand up for themselves and refuse to put up with bad workmanship, poor service, rudeness, and the take-it-or-leave-it attitude.

When writing a letter of complaint, be sure to be specific. Give the facts, not vague generalizations. If it is a product which is not working properly and you have done something to it in an attempt to put it in order, then mention what you have done.

It is pleasant to think that a polite, friendly letter will bring the best results. Unfortunately, however, this is not always the case. There is no doubt that sometimes harsher methods are the only ones which will have any effect. Perhaps one day there will be a change of heart in British trading circles and the attitude that the customer is king will finally prevail.

The few examples which follow are written as if this blissful state of affairs were already in being. The reader is left to concoct his own blistering criticisms, work up his own towering rages, and devise his own diabolical schemes to get the desired reaction out of his erring correspondents.

Opening paragraphs

Dear Sirs,   **377**

      Since installing your Model . . . gas boiler last
January it has broken down three times. Each time we
phoned your local distributor, XYZ, and each time he sent
someone in, made a minor adjustment and lit the boiler
again. Since this has now happened three times in the
space of less than three months, we feel there must be
something radically wrong with the boiler and are therefore
writing direct to you, with a carbon copy to your
distributor.

Dear Mr Green,   **378**

      Since you introduced your new ____ candle electric
light bulb in the spring, we have had so many complaints
from customers about it that we have decided to bring these
complaints to your attention and stop selling the bulb until
the fault has been corrected.

Dear Ms Smith,   **379**

      I really feel I must write to you personally about the
haphazard and unsatisfactory way in which our last order,
No. ____ was filled.

Dear Sirs,   **380**

      As a regular visitor to the ____ Hotel, I am sorry and
disappointed to have to report that during my last visit, just
ended, I found a serious deterioration in the service and an
indifference on the part of the staff which was never
previously characteristic of your establishment.

The body of the letter

381   What happens is simply that the boiler goes out for no apparent reason. Our service man at first simply re-lit it, but when this did no good we got in touch with your distributor, as already mentioned.

The second and third time this happened XYZ said that if it happened again they would have to refer the problem to the manufacturer.

382   Customers complain that the bulbs only last two weeks, a month or two months. We change the bulb for them, only to have them come back again a few weeks later with the same complaint.

383   Here is a detailed list of how this shipment was received:

Box No. 1 . . . . . . One dozen cruets short.
Box No. 2 . . . . . . This whole box consisted of Regency bowls instead of the Clarence ordered.
Box No. 3 . . . . . . This box contained two dozen cake knives which we had not ordered and only four dozen Clarence steak knives and forks, instead of the six we had ordered.
Box No. 4 . . . . . . Two vegetable dishes short.
Box No. 5 . . . . . . One carving set short.
Box No. 6 . . . . . . This box was the only one which contained everything it should and nothing it should not.

384   When I arrived on Sunday evening, March 26, I had to wait a full half hour before getting any attention in the dining room. I realize the waiters are busy, but this kind of service, or rather lack of it, is just not consonant with a first-class hotel. When I finally did get some attention the waiter seemed quite unable to repress his scorn at my failure to order any alcoholic beverage with my meal. It so happens that I am recovering from a long illness and, for the moment, must not indulge in alcohol in any form. However, I do not expect to have to explain this to a waiter to protect myself from his disapproval.

Although I left an order for morning tea on two
different occasions, in each instance I had to go without.

385

Although I arrived at 1.30 p.m. – a reasonable
enough time for lunch, I would have thought – I was told by
the receptionist that I'd better hurry in to lunch as quickly
as possible as 'they stop serving at 2.00 p.m.'.

386

I got the distinct impression that it was up to me to
make things as comfortable as possible for the hotel staff,
rather than the reverse.

Closing paragraphs

We have now reached the stage where we do not
want to wait until 'next time'. We would much prefer you to
send down an engineer who will thoroughly check the
boiler and make the necessary adjustments so that it will
function properly not only for two weeks, but permanently.

387

We look forward to seeing your engineer without
delay.

We cannot help but feel that there must be some fault
in the bulbs and would greatly appreciate your looking into
this. Meanwhile, we are returning our small stock of two
dozen bulbs to you and would be pleased to receive a credit
note for them.

388

389   Obviously, I look forward to receiving the missing items and have already given instructions for the surplus items to be returned to you. However, I am writing in the hope that you will endeavour to improve the situation in your order department.

       This is not the first time that orders have been incorrectly filled and I'm sure you will realize how irritating this is, quite apart from the waste of time involved.

       I hope you will not mind my writing to you so frankly. I value our long-standing business connection very highly and know that, basically, you are extremely anxious to give us good service.

390   I have been staying at the ___ Hotel for so many years that there is nothing I want more than to continue doing so, and I would certainly appreciate your assurance that my last experience was not the result of a new policy, but merely of a set of unfortunate circumstances.

8

Personnel Letters

The letters you write to job applicants and new company employees are very important. In the first place, your letter is often the applicant's first introduction to your company and will, perforce, make an impression of some sort. Whether it is a good, bad or indifferent impression will depend on the appearance and content of the letter, and especially on its tone and attitude. Even if the applicant never gets on your payroll, it is important to leave him or her with a good impression of your company. If you have written him a snooty disdainful letter, if you have spoken down to him, if you have sounded cold and distant, he may well feel disinclined to use your products or your services and may even warn friends and relatives against you in the future.

Applicants who *do* go on your payroll will be entering the most difficult period in the employer–employee relationship – that of induction. Anything you can do to make a new employee feel welcome, to integrate him or her as quickly as possible, will be all to the good. Warm, friendly letters can do a great deal in this direction. Surprisingly enough, almost everything can be said in a warm and friendly way and there is absolutely no reason why a letter setting out working conditions, shop rules, etc. should not be so written.

Letters setting out working conditions, job descriptions, company regulations and so on should also be quite clear and complete in order to avoid misunderstandings and possible disputes. Letters turning down applications should be courteous and diplomatic, and so should other letters which bear unwelcome news.

Letters enclosing application forms, asking applicants to come in for interview, telling that they have, or have not succeeded in getting onto the short list or in securing the position can all be selected from the examples which follow and be committed to the wordprocessor's memory. Then the names, addresses and 'Dear Mr/Ms So-and-So' can be matched in to give each letter that indispensable individually-written look. Job titles and other details can also be inserted by using the machine's editing function.

115

Opening paragraphs

391   Dear Mr Walker,

I am sorry to have to inform you that your application for a position as Trainee Manager with our organization has not been successful.

392   Dear Ms Cooke,

I wish I had better news for you, but unfortunately I am writing to let you know that you have not been successful in your application for a position as Trainee Manager with our organization.

393   Dear Mr Jones,

Thank you for your letter of March 23 in reply to our advertisement for a ____ .

394   Dear Miss Brown,

<u>Multi-lingual Executive Secretary</u>

In accordance with your request, we are happy to enclose an application form for the above position.

395   Dear Miss Brown,

<u>Multi-lingual Executive Secretary</u>

Thank you for your letter of February 22, together with the completed application form regarding the above position.

396   Dear Sir,

We have read with much interest your advertisement in the 'Situations Wanted' column of the <u>Daily Telegraph</u>.

Dear Sir or Madam,   **397**

  Your advertisement in the 'Freelance' column of the
_____ has just been brought to our attention.

Dear Ms Jones,   **398**

  Further to our conversation last Wednesday, I have
now had an opportunity of discussing this matter with our
marketing director, Mr Kenneth Fletcher, and he has asked
me to arrange for him to meet you.

Dear Mr Almond,   **399**

  Thank you for your interesting letter of January 21
regarding the possibility of a vacancy in our company.

Dear Mr Mappin,   **400**

  With reference to our various meetings regarding the
position of sales manager, I should now like to ask you to
come in and meet our managing director, Mr John Silver.

Dear Miss Smith,   **401**

  With reference to your recent application for the
secretarial position with our company, I am very sorry to
have to inform you that your name did not get through to
the short list.

Dear Mr Skinner,   **402**

<u>Area Manager</u>

  With reference to our various meetings in connection
with the above opening, I am very sorry to have to tell you
that, finally, another candidate was selected.

403   Dear Miss Weaver,

You will be pleased to hear that your application has been successful and that we are offering you the secretarial position for which you applied.

404   Dear Mr Grant,

Technical Sales Representative

You will be pleased to hear that you are the successful applicant for the above position and we look forward to welcoming you to our company

405   Dear Mr Campbell,

As agreed yesterday afternoon, I would like to confirm that you will take up your new position with our company on January 2, 1986. Perhaps you will come along to my office first of all.

406   Dear Mr Watson,

Now that all the formalities are completed, I should like to welcome you to Spoonex and tell you how pleased we are that you are joining us.

407   Dear Fellow-Employees,*

I am most anxious that, as members of the company, you should be the first to know the results for the past fiscal year.

408   Dear Fellow-Employees,*

As Christmas approaches and the year draws to a close, I should like to pause to thank you all for your splendid efforts during the year gone by.

---

* In small companies Dear Mr/Mrs/Miss/Ms So-and-So or Dear So-and-So can be written in by hand on each letter.

PERSONNEL LETTERS 119

To all members of the staff:
409

At this time of the year it is customary for all of us
to wonder how big our annual bonus will be. All of us hope
that it will be bigger than it was the year before, but
perhaps few of us stop to think that, being a share of the
profits, if profits are nil, the bonus will likewise be nil.

Dear Fellow-Employees,*
410

This is the kind of letter I very much like writing to
you, although I would prefer to be able to write to each one
of you individually.

Dear Miss Selwyn,
411

You will be pleased to learn that your increase in
salary has been approved and will date from the first of
next month.

Dear Mr Jones,
412

Further to our recent talks, you will be pleased to
hear that I have discussed the question of your promotion
at some length with Mr ____ and we have jointly agreed
that you should take over the position of Northern Area
Manager from March 1 or as soon thereafter as your
successor is ready to take over from you.

Dear Mrs Williams,
413

Once again it is the time of the year when we leave
for a while the cares of business to celebrate Christmas
with our families, and the sole object of this letter is to wish
you and your family a very happy holiday.

---

* In small companies Dear Mr/Mrs/Miss/Ms So-and-So or Dear So-and-So can be written in by
hand on each letter.

414   Dear Jack,

This is just a note to wish you and your family all the very best for Christmas.

415   Dear Mr Merrill,

As you know, we are holding an Open House for customers and neighbours on March 23 to enable them all to see our new premises. Since I believe that company employees should come first, not only in hearing company news but also in enjoying company celebrations, I have decided to hold a staff House Warming party on the previous week, March 18, at 5.30 p.m. or as soon as we 'shut up shop'.

416   Dear Miss Eldridge,

It is my pleasure once again to invite you to our annual Company Dinner Dance.

417   Dear Miss Green,

As you all know, Mr John Howard is retiring at the end of the year. We have decided to hold a surprise party for him on Friday, December 15 at 6 o'clock, in the works' canteen. I shall make it my business to see that Mr Howard is on hand and suspects nothing and I very much hope that you will be able to join us.

418   Dear Ms Simmons,

It is a pleasure to welcome you on Zeeland's management team.

419   Dear Miss Cummings,

I am happy to welcome you to Smithsons & Company.

Dear John,   **420**

   It is a pleasure indeed to send you my hearty
congratulations on your forthcoming wedding.

Dear Mr Willis,   **421**

   I have just learned of your engagement and hasten to
send you my hearty congratulations and best wishes for a
long and happy married life.

Dear Fred,   **422**

   An eight-pound boy they tell me! Hearty
congratulations to you and Jean and best wishes to your
first-born.

Dear Fuller,   **423**

   I have just heard from Miss Skidmore that you have
passed your final examination with flying colours and can
now be considered a fully-fledged Chartered Accountant.

Dear Bill,   **424**

   You will be pleased to learn that you have come out
on top in our Salesman of the Year competition.

Dear Miss Giles,   **425**

   As you have just completed your fifteenth year of
service with the company, you now qualify for membership
to the Golden Circle Club.

Dear Mr Boyle,   **426**
                        <u>Annual check-up</u>
   This is to remind you that your annual medical
check-up at the BUPA Centre is now due.

The body of the letter

427   Perhaps it will help you to feel less disappointed if I tell you that the number of applicants was unusually large and our selection therefore had to be especially stringent. Inevitably <u>some</u> candidates had to be disappointed.

428   Please do not let this result disappoint you too much, or indeed deter you from trying again later on.

429   We were extremely fortunate both in the quantity and quality of the applicants and the result was that, inevitably, some excellent candidates had to be disappointed.

430   I would greatly appreciate your coming in to see me about this opening next Monday, April 30, at 2.30 p.m.

431   Please fill in the attached form and bring it with you when you come.

432   If the date and time mentioned are not suitable, please ring my secretary, Miss Greene, and I'm sure a more suitable appointment can be arranged.

433   Please complete the form and return it to us as soon as possible. We are hoping to draw up a short-list by the end of this month.

434   A short-list will be drawn up in due course and you will, of course, be notified if your name has been included on it.

435   If you would care to telephone my secretary, Mary Wood, she will make an appointment for you to come in and see me about a possible vacancy in our company.

We frequently have small jobs which we feel you might be able to do and I would appreciate your calling Miss Larch, my secretary, for an appointment some time next week. **436**

Next Wednesday at 3.00 p.m. would be a good time, but should this be unsuitable, please give me a ring and I'm sure an alternative day or time can be arranged. **437**

If you would come in any afternoon next week and ask for me, we could discuss the possibility further. **438**

We should like you to start on February 1 and hope you can manage it. Please let us know whether we can expect you then; meanwhile, we would like to congratulate you on your success. **439**

We realize that you will have to give due notice to your present employer and assume this would mean your starting with us on March 1. **440**

You will find Spoonex a very pleasant place to work. It is a company which likes to give full rein to the talent and capacity of its employees, appreciates effort, and rewards achievement. **441**

You will be pleased to learn that it has been a record year. Sales reached the £___ mark for the first time in Company history and profits attained a bumper £___. **442**

I fully realize that such results would not have been possible without the enthusiastic co-operation and effort of each one of you and I want to show my appreciation in tangible form. In the form, in fact, of higher bonuses. **443**

The amount you will get as a bonus is written in ink at the foot of this letter and I hope you will be pleased with it.

444   Just as was the case last year, sales have continued to improve and so have profits. Sales were, in fact, 15 per cent ahead of last year's and profits just fractionally higher than last year.

In view of the very difficult year it has been, these results are most gratifying and I want you to know how very much I appreciate all the hard work you have put in to make them possible.

445   It has been a difficult year in many ways, yet in spite of this, results have been excellent, thanks to the hard work and enthusiasm of all of you.

As you leave for the Christmas holiday, my very good wishes to you and yours go with you. And may the New Year be a happy and prosperous one.

446   Unfortunately, the past year has been a bleak one indeed for our company and, instead of a profit, we have been faced with a loss.

I'm sure you will readily understand that this means there is nothing in the kitty to distribute and that therefore there will be no bonus this year.

This state of affairs is obviously equally disappointing to us all, but we must not permit it to have a demoralizing effect. Business is already on the up-turn and if we all make an effort and work really hard, I am convinced that the current year will show quite different results.

447   Could you come in next Thursday, at 4.00 p.m.?

448   I want you to be the first to know that business has been excellent in the fiscal year just ended: sales were up, profits were up and the future for our company looks very good indeed.

It has, therefore, been possible to increase bonuses accordingly and a very pleasant surprise is in store for you in your next pay packet.

You have worked very hard during the past year and   **449**
I, for one, am extremely pleased to see your efforts suitably
rewarded.

It has been an excellent year for our company and   **450**
you have every right to go off for the holiday break sure in
the knowledge that you have done a good job and well
deserve to enjoy the festivities to the hilt.

It promises to be an extra special event this year, as   **451**
we have managed to get together quite an outstanding floor
show, details of which we are, of course, keeping very
secret.

We shall be presenting our farewell gift to him at the   **452**
party and the set of golf clubs and trolley can now be
viewed in my office any time before December 15.

A man of your personality and drive will certainly do   **453**
well with our company and you will not find us slow either
in recognizing talent and effort or in adequately rewarding
it.

Since you have met the whole of the small team and   **454**
we have all met you, I feel confident we shall all get on well
and work harmoniously together. Certainly you can count
on our wholehearted co-operation and I know we can count
on yours.

A person of your charm, friendly manner, and good   **455**
fashion sense should go far at Smithsons and you will
certainly find no lack of opportunities for advancement.

456   I think you will find this a very pleasant place to work and your colleagues friendly and co-operative.

Ours is an expanding field and, within it, our company holds a pre-eminent position. This means, of course, that there is plenty of scope for our staff to grow with us and take on added responsibilities.

I feel confident that you are just the person to recognize and seize such opportunities as may present themselves and it is a pleasure indeed to have you with us.

457   You will find that we demand dedication and hard work from all our people, but are not ungenerous in rewarding these attributes.

458   My heartiest congratulations to you! I want you to know that we are especially proud to have people like you on the staff and are particularly anxious that you should develop your talents and take on added responsibilities with our company. Let me assure you that you will not find opportunities lacking.

459   I know how hard you have worked to achieve this goal and congratulate you most sincerely on your success.

460   You will be receiving all the more tangible rewards at our sales conference next month, but meanwhile I want to congratulate you on your achievement and tell you how proud I am to have you in our sales team.

461   The announcement will be made officially at our next sales conference and there will also be a surprise in store for you then; meanwhile, let me be the first to congratulate you on this fine achievement.

Ours is an excellent sales team and to be the best person in it is no small achievement. Well done!

You are therefore officially invited to attend its next meeting on Wednesday, March 15 at 6.30 p.m. for 7.00 p.m. You will then be welcomed to the Club and from then on will be part of the élite who have been serving the company for anything up to 25 years! **462**

As you may know, Miss Julie Winslow, who has been with us for just over 25 years, is President of the Club and you will soon be hearing from her. **463**

The sole object of this letter is to put you in the picture and to offer you my sincere congratulations. Our long-service employees are our special pride and it is a pleasure indeed to welcome you to this élite group.

If there are any points which you find unclear, please let me know and we can go over them together. **464**

When you have read the booklet carefully, you will realize that the scheme is a very generous one. **465**

We have made an appointment for you at 3.30 p.m. next Wednesday, March 23. **466**

Please do not feel too dispirited about this outcome, for while four or five candidates for a position are usually on a short list and perhaps two reach the very final stages, ultimately only one of them can be chosen. Inevitably, therefore, there must be three or four disappointed people and one very disappointed one. It does not follow, however, that the latter is necessarily a less able person than the successful candidate, for so many factors enter into personnel selection. **467**

You will find the new position has tremendous scope and offers you every possible opportunity for further advancement. **468**

Closing paragraphs

469   Thank you for attending the interviews and good luck in your attempts to secure a managerial position.

470   Thank you for coming in to see us and please do not be deterred from trying again later on if you so wish.

471   We greatly appreciate your attending the interviews and wish you every success in securing a position in management.

472   I look forward to meeting you.

473   You must not feel that this in any way reflects upon your qualifications or suitability for the position. It is simply a matter of a number of qualified applicants and only one position to fill.

Thank you for coming in to see us.

474   Please confirm this point for us.

475   We hope you will be able to start on February 1 and look forward to hearing from you on this point.

476   Joan Swift is making a note of all those who are able to attend, so please let her know as soon as possible.

477   If ever there are any problems you wish to discuss privately with me, you will always find me readily accessible and prepared to lend a sympathetic ear.

I look forward to your joining us.

478   I look forward to seeing you then.

If we all work together this year as hard as we did **479**
last, results will surely be even better, to the benefit of all of
us.

A Merry Christmas to you, then, and a Happy and **480**
Prosperous New Year.

Keep up the good work! **481**

I would like to wish you every success in your new **482**
position and congratulate you on moving so swiftly up the
ladder of promotion.

Mark the date in your diary and be prepared for a **483**
good time.

Please let Mary Hudson know whether you can come. **484**

May you and your bride enjoy many years of happy **485**
married life.

Let me be the first to congratulate you on achieving **486**
this élite status. As you know, we value our long-service
employees very highly indeed at Longley's.

Please confirm that this appointment is convenient. **487**

Meanwhile, welcome to the club! **488**

9

Making Requests

The main requirement of a letter making a request is that it be clear. If it is not, then it will not have the desired effect. Companies sometimes advertise a number of things, offer more than one booklet, folder, chart or service. If you write in for what is offered, you should clearly specify what you want and not assume that the recipient will know instinctively.

If you want two or more pieces of literature or seek clarification of two or more points, it is helpful to list each one separately and to number them consecutively. This helps the recipient both to see quickly what is wanted and to check each item off the list as he or she puts it into the envelope or writes a reply.

When asking for prices or quotations, it is even more important to be accurate and specific, and to quote the manufacturer's reference number and exact description.

When asking for a charge account to be opened, it saves time to mention any other charge account you may have and who your bankers are.

As to asking for a business appointment, it is important to give sufficient notice and, especially in the case of very busy and important people, to give them as much freedom as possible in the choice of day and time.

Opening paragraphs

489 Dear Sirs,

       I would much appreciate your opening a charge account in my name at your store.

Dear Sirs,   **490**

       We are planning to hold a dealer meeting for about
200 people early next spring and would greatly appreciate
your letting us have the following information:

(1) Type of accommodation you can offer
(2) Price of the various rooms available
(3) Cost of supplying cocktails and snacks for the
    200 guests.

Dear Mr King,   **491**

       Our company is seriously considering opening a
branch in the north of England and there are several
aspects of this operation which I would like to discuss with
you.

Dear Ms Jennings,   **492**

       I shall be in Leeds next Wednesday and Thursday and
am wondering whether I might come in to see you on
either day.

Dear Ms Rhodes,   **493**

       How would you like to cut your billing costs by at
least 20 per cent? Our company has devised a method
whereby you can do just that and eliminate a great deal of
paperwork into the bargain.

Dear Mr Simpson,   **494**

       Would you like to cut your waste to almost nil? I'm
sure you would and I'd like to come in and explain to you
just how you can accomplish this.

Dear Sirs,   **495**

       We are planning to have all our executive offices
modernized and re-decorated and may well decide to turn
the whole operation over to a specialized firm such as
yours.

496   Dear Sirs,

I so frequently need something in a hurry at Jameson's that I feel it would save me a great deal of time if you were to open a charge account in my name. Can you arrange this?

497   Dear Mr Manners,

I am anxious to give my portfolio of American securities a complete overhaul and would greatly appreciate your help in doing so.

498   Dear Miss Giles,

We are seriously considering starting a House magazine and are at the stage of investigating the pros and cons of having the work done outside for us. You were very highly recommended to us by Mr Gimble of Phips, Warner & Peabody and I shculd be much obliged if you will let me have some idea of just how you work and roughly how much we can expect it to cost us.

499   Dear Sirs,

I would greatly appreciate your mailing me the following Management Aids:

(1) Reducing the Risks in Product Development
(2) Traps to Avoid in Small Business Management
(3) Wishing Won't Get Profitable New Products

500   Dear Mr Stone,

I am preparing a talk on marketing for the Young Conservatives and should like to quote from your excellent talk at last month's I.P.A. meeting.

Dear Sirs,   **501**

I would very much appreciate receiving a copy of the booklet A New Look for the Office as advertised in the <u>Daily Telegraph</u>.

Dear Sirs,   **502**

Would you please let us have your quotation for:

1000 cardboard tubes, 4 cm in diameter and 20 cm long.

Dear Sirs,   **503**

We would appreciate your quoting us for maintaining the office grounds.

Dear Sirs,   **504**

Please send us your best quotation for a CAT-245 crawler-mounted shovel.

Dear Sirs,   **505**

Please let us have your most competitive export price for the following machinery to enable us to tender for a Pakistani contract:

15 Go-Go Sheepsfoot tamping Rollers
25 Bronson Rollers

Dear Sirs,   **506**

Can you quote us on the following lots of cork:

25 to 35 bales of <u>Flor</u>
50 to 120 bales of <u>A1</u>
75 to 150 bales of A2 or A3

507   Dear Sirs,

Enclosed is a sketch, drawn to scale, of a small annex we wish to build and for which we already have planning permission. Alongside, you will find listed the materials we wish to use. Would you please let us have your estimate for carrying out this work for us?

508   Dear Ms Monmouth,

Six months have elapsed since your company completed its first language course on our premises and we are now able to appreciate how valuable your instruction has been to our export sales staff.

So satisfied are we, in fact, that we have decided to extend this instruction to several other departments over a period of some months. Would you therefore be good enough to let me know the terms on which you could undertake to run another course for us, followed by yet another, assuming an average of five to six people per course?

509   Dear Sirs,

Pelleting plant

We have to quote for a complete pelleting plant, including transport and erection in Brazil, and would appreciate your letting us have your keenest quotation, including 10 per cent commission for us.

510   Dear Sirs,

We are sending you separately a forged steel part which we require in quantities of approximately 10,000 per month. Would you please let us have your quotation for supplying us with such a part on a regular basis and roughly in the quantities mentioned?

Dear Sirs,   **511**

    We are in the process of redecorating a Board room
for a client and would appreciate your quotation for an
Akusticon ceiling for the room, which measures 10 metres
by 7 metres. The enclosed plan will give you a better idea of
the area involved.

Dear Sirs,   **512**

    Early in the New Year we shall be moving to new
premises in Ealing and want to start off with new furniture
throughout. To give ourselves plenty of time to decide on
our purchases, we would greatly appreciate your sending us
catalogues of your complete line of office furniture.

Dear Sirs,   **513**

    I have been reading with a great deal of interest
about your cellular car phones and would very much like to
have a demonstration of this equipment.

Dear Sirs,   **514**

    Please send me a copy of your brochure Ten Costly
Mistakes to Avoid before You Build, as advertised in the
Financial Times.

Dear Sirs,   **515**

    We are certainly intrigued by your suggestion that
you can save us money by installing your pumping system.
It is indeed true that toffee is not so very different in
consistency from glue, putty or mastics and we would very
much like you to carry out a pumpability test on our
product.

516   Dear Ms Richards,

I attended your preview on Wednesday and was much impressed by the possibilities offered by your Silver Fork service. I wonder if you would care to come and discuss this service with my Personnel Manager and me in greater detail?

517   Dear Sirs,

We are considering computerising our accounts department and would greatly appreciate your sending us some preliminary information on your Series 200 computer, together with details of your rental/purchase plan.

518   Dear Sirs,

Please send me details of your attitude surveys and, if possible, a short list of British companies which have made use of your services.

519   Dear Sirs,

We understand that you do historical and other background research on almost any subject and are wondering whether you could submit a quotation for a research job on cosmetics throughout the ages. We realize this is a vast field and suggest you quote us for the complete job in depth, with an alternative quotation for a much briefer version, running to, say, 50 pages.

520   Dear Sirs,

Our firm is trying to track down information on behalf of a client and we believe your back-dated clipping service would be invaluable to us in this task.

Dear Sirs, **521**

Could you please quote us a CIF London price on the following Travertine marble tables:

100 coffee tables measuring approximately 1 m by 80 cm
100 round coffee tables, approximate diameter 1 m
 50 dining tables, approximately 1.5 m by 1m

The body of the letter

My bankers are Barclays Bank PLC, Waterloo Branch, **522** and I have a charge account with Dunhill's, Piccadilly.

I cannot refer you to any other store, since I am not **523** in the habit of opening accounts, but you can certainly refer to the Midland Bank PLC, St James's Street Branch, as well as to the Bank of London & South America, Leadenhall Street.

Could I come and see you sometime next Thursday? I **524** shall be arriving in town at 9.00 a.m. sharp and could make yours my first call. If this is not convenient, however, please let me know as I could easily rearrange my day and come in later in the morning.

Would you be good enough to spare me a little of your **525** time next Wednesday afternoon or the following morning? I shall be arriving in Leeds around noon and hope to leave as soon as possible on the Thursday.

If you will let me know what time is most **526** convenient, I will arrange my day accordingly.

May I come along and tell you more about our **527** remarkable system and how it could help you?

I shall be in your neighbourhood next Wednesday **528** afternoon and could come in at any time to suit you.

529   I am usually in your area every other Thursday and am hoping that you can spare me a little of your time on Thursday, March 25. I am sure you will find it time well spent.

530   To help us to reach a decision we should like to have, first of all, some general information on how you operate, how much it is likely to cost us and so on.

If you have any suitable literature, we would very much like to study it; otherwise perhaps you could send someone along to see us.

531   However, a great many of our top executives have definite ideas on how they want their offices decorated and a certain amount of tact will be needed to reconcile individual tastes with an overall scheme.

532   The room would need to be large enough to accommodate not only the 200 guests, plus about a dozen of us, but also about five display units and five stands. We should also need plenty of electric light points to light up the displays adequately.

533   Perhaps you would let me see two or three alternative menus with corresponding prices.

534   Perhaps the best plan would be to run a bar, but I leave it to you to suggest the most practical arrangement for the number of people involved.

535   We have an in-house magazine in mind and would need about a thousand copies of each issue. Whether it should be a monthly or a weekly we have not yet decided, neither have we given much thought to format. In fact, our plans are still very much in the formative stage.

We are thinking tentatively of having two editions, **536**
one internal and the other external, some of the material,
including some of the actual sheets, being common to both
editions.

In the final analysis, cost will greatly influence our **537**
decision and we would particularly like you to give us a
rough idea of what this might be.

I understand there is no charge for these admirable **538**
'Aids', but should I be mistaken, please let me know and I
will send you a cheque without delay.

Do you happen to have a script of the talk and, if so, **539**
may I borrow it? You may be sure that I will take the
greatest care of it.

Perhaps you would be good enough to address it to **540**
me personally to ensure that it reaches my desk.

The tubes should be sealed at one end and have a **541**
removable top at the other.

The grounds cover half an acre and consist of two **542**
small lawns in the front of the building, two large ones at
the back, shrubs around the sides, two rose beds, paths and
very little else.

If you would like to see the grounds, by all means **543**
come along any time and ask for me.

Please also give us your best delivery date. We need **544**
this equipment urgently.

545 The price should be FOB Port of London, including export packing. We expect competition to be very keen indeed for this contract and therefore urge you to calculate your price very accurately, allowing a 3 per cent commission for us.

546 Prices should be CIF London or Felixstowe.

547 FOB Spanish port would suit us quite well.

548 We are hoping to move into the new annexe by next spring and would therefore urge you to give this matter your prompt attention.

549 If you wish to come over and see the site, please let us know.

550 We think that your Model 'K' plant would be the most suitable for this particular case, since the clients want to produce ____ kilos of pellets a day.

551 Your quotation should also include the cost of an engineer going to Bahia, supervising the erection, training the operators and putting the plant smoothly into operation.

552 Please separate each item clearly in your quotation, so that we know the exact amount of each. Our client may well decide to erect the plant and put it into operation himself, although we shall endeavour to dissuade him from doing this.

553 If it proves as useful as it sounds, we might well decide to equip all our executives with one.

I shall be in the office all next week, with the **554**
exception of Wednesday, so perhaps you would call my
secretary, Miss Greene, to arrange a mutually convenient
appointment.

Please let me know what you need in order to carry **555**
out such a test. Do we send you a sample of our product, or
would you need to visit our plant and see how our present
operation works?

If you will give me a ring, we can perhaps arrange a **556**
meeting some time next week.

I would also be interested to learn just how you carry **557**
out these surveys, whether they involve keeping staff away
from their work and, if so, how long for, and so on.

I would also like to know roughly how much these **558**
surveys cost, bearing in mind that our company has about
500 employees, divided into three branches.

We would also like to have the names of two or three **559**
British or American companies who have used your
services in the past.

Do you also give guidance on how to use the material **560**
you supply for Public Relations purposes?

We feel that the material you collect could be very **561**
useful for a number of purposes, other than the one we
have in mind. Could you, without breach of confidence, let
us know the purposes for which some of your other clients
use this material?

The client in question, Mr John F. Stoddard, operated **562**
a company called Bearings & Castings Inc., in St. Paul,
Minnesota between 1970 and 1974 and we would like to see
any newspaper clipping about this company or Mr
Stoddard.

563 We are looking for any reference to a Mr Louis H. Ferris and his marriage to a Miss Marylin Skinner, or indeed to anyone else. Such references might have occurred any time between 1960 and the early 1970s.

This might be a difficult one to track down, but we should be grateful for any information you can trace. Such items might have appeared in Canadian, South African or European newspapers.

564 Please also let us know your best delivery date.

565 You will, of course, appreciate that this research is of a very confidential nature and we are sure we may rely upon you to keep it so.

566 Meanwhile, I am enclosing testimonials from several companies which have adopted our system. You will notice that one of the most enthusiastic among them is in your own line of business.

Closing paragraphs

567 I look forward to hearing from you.

568 I do hope you can arrange this for me.

569 If there is any other information you need, please let me know.

570 I look forward to meeting you (or seeing you, as the case may be).

571 I will telephone you as soon as I arrive.

572 I will telephone your secretary in a couple of days and arrange a convenient time.

We look forward to your early reply.   **573**

If you need any further information before quoting   **574**
us on a suitable plant, please let us know.

This could prove to be a very interesting order for   **575**
both our companies and we look forward to hearing from
you soon.

If you will phone my secretary, Miss Taylor, she will   **576**
arrange a mutually convenient appointment.

We very much look forward to trying this equipment.

. I look forward with great interest to hearing from   **577**
you.

Would you please let us know whether you can   **578**
undertake this task and what your fees would be?

We look forward to hearing from you.

10

Placing Orders

One of the easiest of business letters to write is the one ordering goods or services. Its only requirement is that it be clear, explicit, and complete. In other words, it should contain full details of the merchandise ordered, such as manufacturer's name or number, size, colour, voltage, horse power or whatever. It should indicate the price you expect to pay or have previously agreed on, the delivery date and delivery instructions.

In many instances, placing an order is simply a question of accepting a quotation, an estimate or a *proforma* invoice. In many other cases, it involves sending in an order form supplied either by the manufacturer or by the company placing the order, with or without a covering letter, while in other cases special order cards are used.

The examples which follow cover only such orders as involve writing a letter. The number of letters given is, of necessity, far less than those on other subjects, since placing orders does not offer such a variety of different approaches.

Opening paragraphs

579   Dear Sirs,

<u>Four-wheel drive Pearson lorries for</u>
<u>Paraguay</u>

With reference to the above transaction, you will be pleased to learn that we have succeeded in securing this interesting order and consequently accept your Pro Forma Invoice No. 4761 dated July 26, 1985.

144

Dear Mr Gibbons,   **580**

We have carefully studied your estimate for building the annex to our factory and have decided to ask you to go ahead with the work.

Dear Sirs,   **581**

Thank you for your quotation for the cardboard tubes dated September 25. We find this quite satisfactory and are enclosing our official order form for the tubes as quoted.

Dear Ms Roberts,   **582**

This is to confirm our telephone conversation of this morning when I told you we had decided to go ahead and have the Board room redecorated in accordance with your recommendations and estimate.

Dear Miss Simmons,   **583**

We have now had an opportunity of carefully studying your proposals for streamlining our paperwork and have decided to go ahead with the programme you outline.

Dear Mr Wells,   **584**

Many thanks for your lucid outline of the work you propose to do for us and your two alternative estimates. We have decided to go ahead on the shorter version, 'Plan B', for which you quote us a price of £420.

Dear Mr Hawkins,   **585**

Decentralization plan

We have given your proposal for decentralizing our operation considerable thought and have finally decided to go ahead with it, exactly as outlined by you.

586   Dear Ms White,

Thank you for your detailed letter of March 14. We agree with you that your service is just what we need and would like you to go right ahead with the research job on Mr John F. Saunders, as outlined in our previous letter.

587   Dear Ms Richards,

Further to our various meetings and correspondence in connection with your Silver Fork Service, we have decided to adopt it in our works for a trial period of six months on the terms outlined in your letter of March 21.

588   Dear Mr Greene,

Series 200 Computer

Further to our exchange of correspondence and your visit here last month, we have decided to install the above machine on your rental/purchase plan.

589   Dear Mr King,

Job No. 25689

Our plans for redecorating the Board room have finally been fixed and we have decided to go ahead and use your Akusticon Ceiling, as per your Quotation No. 56 dated July 1.

590   Dear Ms Smedley,

You will be pleased to learn that we have decided to use 'K' furniture throughout our new building and are enclosing our official Order No. 147 covering all the items needed.

Dear Mr Young,   **591**

   After giving considerable thought to the possibility of
equipping every sales representative's car with your
cellular car phones, we have decided to get this equipment
initially only for our Southern Area. If in a few months'
time we are convinced that it was a worthwhile investment,
we shall then order the phones for the remaining two sales
areas.

   Would you please, therefore, enter our order for:

   12 XYZ Cellular Car Phones @ £____ each, including
   cost of installation.

Dear Sirs,   **592**

   Please enter our order for the following:

1. 10 Finished Shutters, 27 (white), 60 cm wide,
    75 cm high at £6.50 ea .... £ 65.00
2. 10 Finished Shutters, 4 (Capri blue),
    38 cm wide, 50 cm high at £4.50 ea 45.00
3. 10 Whitewood Shutters, 30 cm wide,
    60 cm high at £2.00 ea 20.00
                                                   ─────────
                                                   £130.00

Dear Sirs,   **593**

                    Fork-lift trucks for India
   You will be glad to learn that we were successful
bidders for the above contract and are now pleased to
enclose our Order No. Ex-5758 based on your Pro Forma
Invoice No. 7583 dated January 21, 1985.

Dear Sirs,   **594**

   Will you please let us have three copies of 'Better
Business Letters' by J.W. Steward at £15.00 each post paid?

The body of the letter

595   Enclosed is our covering order. As originally stated, the lorries must reach Paraguay by the end of March; consequently there is no time to be lost in preparing them for shipment.

The M.V. 'Morning Star' sails from Felixstowe for Buenos Aires on February 1 and we rely on you to do everything you can to have the lorries ready for loading then.

596   From our point of view, there is no reason why you should not begin at once and we look forward to hearing when you can make a start. As you will recall, we want to be able to move in, lock stock and barrel, by early April at the latest.

597   We would like to have the tubes by May 20, if at all possible, and hope you will do your best to get them to us by then.

598   Please let me know as soon as possible when you plan to begin the work. We are naturally anxious to have everything in order for the first Board meeting after the summer holidays.

599   We feel that it would be a good idea for Mr Saunders to begin his work in the general office during the summer when things are quieter and hope you will have no difficulty in arranging for him to come in on Monday, July 31, or the following Monday.

600   The week of May 21 would be a good one for the pilot session and the two workshops to follow could be held two weeks later.

601   Please let me know whether you can move the equipment in by June 1, so that I may inform the staff accordingly.

I understand that you can begin the service at any   **602**
time and, this being so, I would like it to run from May 1.

I gather there is a delivery delay of 2 to 3 months on   **603**
the equipment, but would appreciate your doing what you
can to reduce it as much as possible.

As we would prefer to install the new system during   **604**
the quieter summer weeks, we do not in the least mind
waiting until the end of July for this equipment, but would
appreciate your letting us have a definite delivery date.

We are most anxious to have all the furniture in   **605**
place by May 31, so that we can make a smooth change-
over during the week-end.

We understand you can deliver these shutters from   **606**
stock and look forward to receiving them very soon.

Please let us know your earliest delivery date on this   **607**
material.

This merchandise is very urgently needed and we ask   **608**
you to make a special effort to get it to us at the earliest
possible moment.

We look forward to hearing when you can make   **609**
delivery.

The contract calls for delivery by March 15, 1986,   **610**
which means the trucks will have to leave your works early
in February. We cannot impress on you too strongly the
importance of observing this delivery clause, as the Indian
Government have every right to refuse delivery of the
machines if they do not arrive by the date specified.

Enclosed is our cheque for £12.00 to cover cost.   **611**

612   Please bill us accordingly.

613   Please send the package COD.

Closing paragraphs

614   Please let us know when the lorries are ready and we will then give you shipping marks and further instructions.

615   Please let us hear from you soon.

616   Please confirm delivery date.

617   Please let us know whether this will be in order.

618   Perhaps you would give me a ring so that we may fix definite dates for the sessions.

619   I look forward to hearing from you on this point.

620   We hope there will be no difficulty about this and look forward to your confirmation.

621   Shipping marks and shipping instructions will follow shortly.

11

Making Announcements

When making announcements, especially to the staff, a great many companies adopt the tones of the autocrat and sometimes even resort to sarcasm and attempts at intimidation. At best, announcements are couched in mandarin language seemingly aimed at concealing their meaning. A priceless example of how *not* to compose an announcement is the following notice proudly displayed above the fire-extinguishing buckets of water by a small manufacturer who must remain nameless:

THESE BUCKETS ARE NOT MEANT FOR FAG-ENDS

Anyone with any spirit at all would obviously react by throwing in as many cigarette-butts as he could possibly get hold of. The compiler of this pearl of wisdom obviously knew nothing at all about human psychology. He belonged to an age happily passed and still thought that people could be driven, if not by whips, then by sarcasm.

The moral is, of course, that if you want instructions followed, rules obeyed, admonitions heeded, then eschew the dictatorial manner, resist the temptation to be sarcastic, *ask* people to do things, ask pleasantly and, if at all possible, tell them why.

Of course, not all announcements are concerned with rules and regulations and not all are addressed to staff. Some are sent in the form of a letter to customers and suppliers. Others are fixed to the bulletin board and deal with annual closure, change of working hours, new social benefits, and so on.

Whatever their subject matter and their audience, announcements should be written in a pleasant and readable style and should not sound like 'Superior Orders'.

Since a great many announcements are not written in the form of a letter, the examples which follow are not divided in the same way as the rest of the book, but grouped under subject matter. Each paragraph is numbered so that it can be coupled with any other pertinent paragraph. Where necessary you can add your own 'To our customers', 'To all members of the staff', 'Dear colleagues', or whatever the situation calls for. Likewise, there is nothing to prevent you from ending some of the announcements in the same way as a letter, if the situation calls for it.

Working hours, holidays and benefits

622   You will be pleased to learn that, as from June 3, 1986, working hours will be modified as follows:

Factory: Monday to Friday 8.30 a.m. to 5.00 p.m.
Office: Monday to Friday 9.00 a.m. to 5.30 p.m.

623   You will be pleased to learn that we are to begin the New Year with a slightly shorter working week. The new hours are as follows:

Works: Monday to Thursday 8.30 a.m. to 5.00 p.m.
         Friday 8.00 a.m. to 4.00 p.m.

Office: Monday to Friday 9.30 a.m. to 5.30 p.m.

The new hours will begin on Thursday, January 2, 1986.

624   Any hourly-paid worker continuing after 5.00 p.m. Monday to Thursday or after 4.00 p.m. on a Friday, will do so at the overtime rate. However, no one is to work overtime without having been expressly asked to do so by the foreman.

625   As you will no doubt gather, the new hours mean that the working week is reduced to ____ hours for office staff and to ____ for people in the works.

626   When the new hours are introduced, we shall try to confine overtime work to two hours a day, from 5.00 p.m. to 7.00 p.m., and no one will be asked to work overtime on Fridays.

627   From the same date, overtime will only be worked in exceptional cases.

628   We are sure you will all welcome the extra leisure, even though it is only half an hour a day.

Annual close-down   629

This year our works will close down for the two
weeks beginning July 24 and 31.

If you have any urgent orders, therefore, we urge you
to let us have them at the earliest possible moment to
enable us to put them through before the holiday.

Annual close-down   630

We are giving you hereunder a list of annual close-
down dates for our various suppliers to enable you to take
the necessary action with regard to future orders:

Company 'A'. . . . . weeks beginning August 1 and 8
Company 'B'. . . . .   "   "   August 8 and 15
Company 'C'. . . . . week beginning August 1
Company 'D'. . . . . weeks beginning July 15 and August 1

Our works will remain open all summer as usual but,
as most of our suppliers will be closed at least part of the
month of August, it would be helpful if you could let us
know in advance whether you are likely to have any
unusually large orders before the end of the summer.

Summer holidays, 1986   631

Will you please let me know as soon as possible
when you would like to take your holidays this year?

The holiday period runs from ____ to ____ and only in
exceptional circumstances can anyone be allowed to be
away after ____.

Summer holidays, 1986   632

The enclosed grid covers every week in the holiday
period, which runs from May 1 to August 31. Will you
please put a cross in the weeks you would like to select for
your holiday and return the grid to me as soon as possible?

Compatibly with the smooth running of each   633
department, we will do our very best to give everyone the
dates preferred.

634

Holiday entitlement

All employees who have been on the staff three complete years or more are entitled to four weeks' holiday this year. Other employees are entitled to the following:

Six months' employment ...... 1 week's holiday
One full year .... 2 weeks' holiday
Two full years .... 3 weeks' holiday

635

Holiday entitlement

You will be pleased to learn that, starting this year, all employees with two or more years' service will be entitled to three weeks' holiday a year. Anyone having joined between ____ and ____ will be entitled to two weeks, and anyone who has been with us for six months will be entitled to one week's holiday.

636

In due course you will be receiving a form from your department head on which you can indicate the dates you would like to take.

637

Enclosed is the new booklet explaining the Company Pension Scheme. It has been brought up to date and completely rewritten to make it more easily understood and more readable.

You will find it contains information vital to you and your family.

638

We have spent considerable time devising a non-contributory pension scheme to give you all the best possible protection the company can afford and the enclosed booklet explains it to you in detail.

639

As from January 2, the company is taking out a group life insurance policy to cover all employees with six months' service or more. Will you please be sure to call at Miss ____'s office to fill in the appropriate form, nominating a beneficiary and so on.

Internal organization

640 Arrangements have been made for all members of the staff to take their midday meal in the canteen of our sister-company, ____. Meals are served from 12.00 noon to 2.00 p.m. and anyone wanting to take advantage of this facility has only to go along, without need for any formality.

641 You will be pleased to know that our company has worked out an agreement with ____, next door to us, for all members of our staff to take a hot midday meal in their canteen.

If you wish to take advantage of this facility, please pick up a meal card at the Personnel Office.

642 You will be pleased to learn that we have decided to open our own canteen on the top floor of the building.

Morning and afternoon tea will be served there, as well as lunch.

We hope you will all enjoy this new facility.

643 In view of the gradual increase in the number of employees and also because two or more hours of overtime are so frequently worked, we have decided that, beginning next Monday, March 2, lunch and light hot snacks will be served in the canteen, instead of only tea and cold snacks.

The available space is being increased, but this will take a little time and, meanwhile, things will be somewhat cramped.

In due course, however, you will no doubt find the expansion of the canteen service a boon.

644 We have decided to install two beverage machines on each floor and to eliminate the tea trolleys. This will mean that you can go up to the machine at any time and get a cup of tea, coffee or chocolate, instead of waiting for the tea trolley to come around.

645
To avoid the usual congestion and resultant waste of time at the tea bars, we have decided that morning and afternoon tea breaks will be taken in two sessions, at the following times:

| Morning break: | 10.00 a.m. and 10.10 a.m. |
| Afternoon break: | 3.00 p.m. and 3.10 p.m. |

If your surname begins with a letter in the first part of the alphabet, A–L, please take the first session. If you belong in the M–Z group, then please take the second break.

We do not wish to appear dogmatic about this and prevent two people who particularly want to have tea together from doing so. We simply ask you to add commonsense to flexibility; so if you see the counter jam-packed, take the next session.

646
Office overalls

Any member of staff who would like to wear an overall in the office to protect her street clothing will be issued one by the company free of charge. Please apply to the Personnel Office.

647
Protective gloves

It does not appear to be generally known that the company issues disposable plastic gloves for use when carrying out some of the messier operations in the reprographics department.

If you would like a supply of these protective gloves, simply put in a requisition on the office stationery form.

648
Company hairdresser

You will be pleased to learn that our good neighbours ____ have kindly offered to extend the services of their company hairdresser to all our female employees.

If you want your hair done, all you have to do is go into the hairdressing room on the first floor and make an appointment. Charges are very moderate.

Wages and salaries   **649**

As a result of the poll taken among all company
employees, we have decided to pay wages and salaries by
cheque, beginning the first pay day in January for manual
workers and January 31 for monthly-paid employees.

Wages and salaries   **650**

For security reasons, and in agreement with
everyone on the payroll, we have decided to pay all wages
and salaries by credit transfer, beginning with the first pay
day in June.

This will mean that your wage or salary will be
deposited direct into your bank account by our Chief
Accountant. You will, of course, still get your usual pay slip
giving details of deductions and so on.

Please fill in the name and address of your bank on
the enclosed form and return it to Mr ____'s office without
delay. Any employee not having a bank account should see
Mr ____ right away.

651   <u>Office stationery</u>

Within the next few days, every department will be issued with the new company stationery, which has been especially designed in the new House style.

The stationery will consist of:

1. A.4-size letterheads, to be used for average-length letters
2. A continuation sheet, also in A.4-size
3. A.5-size letterheads, to be used for short letters. This size is exactly half the size of the A.4
4. A.4-size internal memorandum sheets
5. A.5-size internal memorandum sheets
6. A.4-size invoice forms
7. A.5-size invoice forms
8. A compliments slip.
9. A.4-size order forms
10. A.5-size order forms
11. Envelopes of suitable size

Will you please return any old stationery supplies to Stores in exchange for your new supplies?

The new stationery will be used throughout the company beginning Monday, July 2.

652   <u>Placing orders</u>

From June 2, Mr Peter Parrish will be in charge of placing all orders on behalf of the company. Would you please therefore pass along all your requirements to him rather than ordering direct as in the past?

Placing orders   **653**

As you all know, our Buying Department has now been in operation for almost a year. Unfortunately, however, many of us are still guilty of placing the occasional order direct with a supplier.

I realize how hard it is to break a habit of long standing, but I'm sure you will appreciate that one of the reasons for having a buyer is to enable the company to obtain supplies at the best possible price. It is the buyer's job to negotiate purchases on behalf of the company. If you order direct, you are preventing him from doing his job, perhaps paying more than necessary and taking time away from doing your own job.

I therefore count on you to resist the temptation of ordering direct and to put all your requirements through John Brown's office in future.

We are enclosing a revised drawing of the ___   **654**
assembly, including the new part numbers. As you will notice, this improved design eliminates a few parts and we would therefore appreciate your going by the new drawing and using the new numbers when ordering.

In order to improve deliveries, we have decided in   **655**
future to have the ___ you order from us sent to you direct from our Italian supplier. All the other components will, of course, continue to be shipped to you from the United Kingdom.

We feel this arrangement will result in your getting a faster service from us.

You will be pleased to learn that, as from January   **656**
11, 1986, we shall be delivering your orders in our own fleet of vans. This will greatly speed up delivery, as orders will no longer have to wait around for the carrier to call.

We are happy indeed to be able to offer you this improved service.

657   To give you quicker service, we have decided to deliver all orders coming from the north of England direct from our Leeds works.

We would therefore appreciate your addressing all future orders direct to our Leeds office, at 55 St. Leonard's Street.

Safety and health measures

Although safety posters can be bought or hired, there is frequently a need to compose your own warnings or admonitions on matters of safety.

658   In the interests of your own safety, the company has decided to issue every man with a small bottle of goggle-cleaning fluid and a wad of tissues. You should keep this cleaning material in your overall pocket, so that it is handy to use whenever your goggles are dirty.

This safety measure is being taken because far too many men are working without goggles on the pretext that they are dirty and they 'haven't got around to cleaning them yet'.

Do bear in mind that your eyes are your most precious possession. You would never forgive yourself if they were damaged through neglect or laziness on your part.

WEAR YOUR GOGGLES. KEEP THEM CLEAN.

659   Please remember that fire regulations demand that the four doors on this floor be kept clear and accessible all the time.

If a fire were to break out, you would not have time to remove the pile of old box files which has been standing in front of one of the doors for the past few weeks.

Remember: FIRES CAN HAPPEN! It is up to you to do all you can to ensure your own and your colleagues' safety by following the fire regulations.

One or two people have been found having a quick **660**
smoke in the paint shop. These people are obviously so
irresponsible that they do not mind jeopardizing their
colleagues' safety in order to indulge their irresistible urge.

Smoking in the paint shop is VERY DANGEROUS and
must never be done.

Please remember that, in the interests of safety, **661**
smoking can only be permitted outside the laboratories. You
MUST stub your cigarette out BEFORE you re-enter the lab.

We realize that it is soothing to be able to smoke
while carrying out experiments, but it can also have
disastrous results, as you all know so well.

'Flu jabs   **662**

This year again the company is making 'flu 'jabs'
available to every employee who wants one.

If you would like to take this preventive measure,
please let Miss Adams know right away.

'Flu epidemic   **663**

Every employee wishing to have a preventive
injection against the current influenza epidemic should
report immediately to the sick-bay.

Company doctor   **664**

Please note that Doctor Williams will be in
attendance at the sick-bay every Wednesday afternoon,
between 2 and 4 o'clock. If you need to see him, just go
along. No appointment is necessary.

This new time-table will go into effect on June 1.

Sick-bay   **665**

As from July 1, the sick-bay is being moved to larger
quarters on the fourth floor. Sister Sullivan will be in
attendance there, as usual, every day.

666   Training in First-Aid

In order to keep up the numbers of staff trained in
first-aid, we have decided to offer a further opportunity for
training to any member of staff who cares to volunteer.

Training takes place at the St. John's Ambulance
Industrial First-Aid Unit in London Road and lasts a week.

Anyone wishing to volunteer for the course should
notify Stella Riggs as soon as possible.

667   First-aid

Not everyone is aware that the Red Cross hut on the
Trading Estate is open to all tenants and their employees. If
ever you should need treatment, you have only to go over
there. The hut is open every day from 9.30 a.m. to 12.00
noon and from 2.30 p.m. to 4.00 p.m.

Other rules and regulations

668   A very enthusiastic member of the staff decided to
work late one day last week but, when attempting to leave
the office just before 8.00 p.m., found that she was locked in.

The last thing we want to do is stop anyone staying
on to finish urgent work, but we do urge you to let Mr ____
know if you intend to do so. He is the last person to leave
and locks all doors at 7.30 p.m. Certainly everyone else
should normally be out by that time, but if in exceptional
circumstances you do not think you will be, then please
notify him.

669   I occasionally walk through a department during
lunch time and find there is not a soul at his or her desk.
I have even had to answer a telephone left unattended.

This is obviously not good enough and I would
appreciate all department heads making sure that clerical
and secretarial staff take turns at lunch, so that there is
always at least one person in the department all through
the lunch hour.

Lunch breaks   **670**

The rule about staggering lunch seems to have been sagging to the point that the chairman has had to complain about offices being empty during the lunch hour.

As you all know, lunch should be taken either from 12.00 noon to 1.00 p.m. or from 1.00 p.m. to 2.00 p.m. Please put your name on the attached schedule under the hour you prefer and return it to me. The final schedule will eventually go up on the bulletin board and anyone wishing to change a lunch hour for any reason should arrange to do so with a colleague, not simply change his or her time without providing for a replacement.

Will you all please make sure that your windows are   **671**
properly closed before you leave the office at night? This is even more important when you stay late.

Please remember that the Stationery Supply Office is   **672**
only open Mondays and Wednesdays. Only in cases of real emergency should you expect exceptions to be made.

Appointments, promotions and retirements

You will be pleased to learn that Mr P.C. Daniels has   **673**
been appointed managing director of the company as from January 2, 1986. I am sure you will all give Mr Daniels the same loyal support and co-operation which you gave to Mr Owens during his tenure of office.

I'm sure you will all be pleased to learn that, as from   **674**
January 2, 1986, Mr William B. Hopkins will be taking over as managing director, while Mr Edward A. Philips will step into Mr Hopkins' shoes as marketing director.

Other changes will follow and you may be sure that you will be the first to know about them.

675   The promotion of Mr David Mathews to the position of marketing manager has brought about a number of other promotions, namely:

> Mr Donald Seymour becomes sales manager for the London area
> Mr Ronald Wilkins becomes area manager, Southern Region
> Miss Joan Fleming becomes sales supervisor, London area.

676   You will be pleased to learn that Mr Arthur J. Woodstock has been appointed company secretary. Other senior appointments will follow in anticipation of the planned expansion.

677   This is to let you know that on September 1 Miss Belinda Black will be joining us as public relations officer. She will be telling you about her appointment herself and explaining to you what she will be doing. Public relations is a rather misunderstood function, but an extremely important one none the less, as Belinda herself will no doubt explain to you.

678   You will be pleased to learn that, following my appointment as general sales manager, the position of export manager is being taken over by Miss Rollins, my former assistant, whom you already know.

      You therefore need have no fears that your orders will not be taken care of as before. Furthermore, if I can be of any assistance to you in my new position, I shall be only too glad to do so.

679   I should like you all to know that Miss Elizabeth Winslow, who has been my most efficient and patient personal secretary for the past 15 years, is to retire on June 30.

      I know that I shall not be the only one to miss her, for her efficiency, cheerfulness and co-operative spirit are known and appreciated by all.

My imminent retirement has certainly been the   **680**
worst-kept secret ever. Yet I want to tell you all officially
that I shall be retiring at the end of the year and passing
the company reins over to Mr John Stevens.

This is to let you know that I shall be retiring at the   **681**
end of June and that the new manager of this branch will
be Mr Richard Scott.

I would like you to know how very much I have
enjoyed our association during the many years we have
been doing business together.

I would like you to know that I shall be retiring from   **682**
the company at the end of this year. Between now and then
I shall be making the rounds with my successor, Miss Judy
White, whom I'm sure you'll find a very likeable person.

Social activities

River trip   **683**

Coaches will be leaving the factory at 8.00 a.m. sharp
next Sunday, August 2, for our annual outing.

Do please all make a point of arriving in plenty of
time, since the coaches MUST leave at 8.00 a.m. if we are to
catch the connection with the river steamer.

See you all aboard with cameras, guitars and sun tan
lotion!

Annual outing   **684**

As usual this year, we are having to plan well ahead
for the annual outing because of the transport problem.

Will all staff needing transport please write their
name clearly in the right-hand column below, and all those
offering seats in their cars put their name and number of
seats offered in the left-hand column?

We will then match up the two columns and hire
additional transport to take care of the overspill.

685   <u>Annual outing</u>

We have decided this year to hire coaches for the
outing and all go together, since many car owners felt they
would prefer the 'day off' from driving and relax with the
rest of us.

Will all those who plan to come on the outing
therefore put their names below (block letters, please!)?.

686   <u>Annual outing</u>

There has been a strong feeling for the past couple of
years that we ought to make a change from the usual trip
to the seaside and have a dinner-dance instead.

Obviously, it is quite impossible to please everyone,
but since the seaside faction have been having their way for
so long, we have decided this year to let the dinner-dancers
have their innings.

So a dinner-dance it will be. We shall have it at the
river-side restaurant called the 'White Fox' at Maidenhead
on Saturday, August 20, and coaches will be laid on to take
us all there and bring us back again.

All those wishing to come along please let Sally Miles
know right away.

Christmas party   687

As usual, we urge you this year to leave your car at home and join everybody else in the coaches which will take us to and from the Christmas party.

It is being held this year at the 'Horse and Hounds' and the coaches – two of them – will be making the following stops:

```
Leave the Works.................... 7.30 p.m.
Leave Wickley Corner.............. 7.40 p.m.
Leave Cross Common .............. 7.45 p.m.
Arrive 'Horse and Hounds'......... 8.00 p.m.
```

There will be a choice of two coaches leaving the party: 11.30 p.m. for those wishing to leave early. 1.00 a.m. for those wishing to stay to the very end.

Return coaches will also stop at Wickley Corner and Cross Common.

Christmas dinner-dance   688

As you all know, we are meeting in the Palm Court of the Waldorf Hotel at 6.45 p.m. on Wednesday, December 21, for our annual dinner-dance.

Anyone wishing to go home to change beforehand may leave the office at 4.00 p.m.

Christmas 1985   689

Both factory and offices will close down at 1 o'clock on Friday, December 24, and will reopen on Tuesday morning, January 2. Please gather around in my office for a Christmas 'noggin' before you leave on Friday.

Christmas lunch   690

A Christmas lunch of turkey, plum pudding and all the trimmings will be served in the canteen on Thursday, December 23. Will all those wishing to partake sign their name beneath this notice? Will groups who wish to sit together please give clear indications and a suitable table will be arranged for them.

General announcements

691   <u>Word-processing centre</u>

The new word-processing centre will come into operation next Monday, March 23. Its operation is simplicity itself. If you want to dictate some letters, all you do is pick up your telephone receiver and dial '41'. You will then be connected to the dictating equipment and can start dictating your correspondence without further ado.

The letters will then be typed by whichever operator happens to be free and she will bring the finished letters to you when they are ready.

While some of the word-processing operators were previously attached to a particular department or executive, please bear in mind that you must not claim any particular operator as your own. Neither must you attempt to enlist the operator's help with non-typing tasks.

While some executives will no doubt feel that they have lost a certain amount of prestige by not having a typist to call their own, I hope you will all realize that the new arrangement will result in far more efficiency, better use of time and greater fairness in the availability of help to all who need it.

As you all know, if Britain is successfully to compete **692**
in world markets she must become more efficient. The dead
wood must go, operations must be streamlined, we must
become lithe, flexible, up to date.

All of this applies equally to us as a company vitally
interested in the export markets and we do not intend to be
left behind for want of proper humility.

Next Monday, therefore, some gentlemen from the
consulting firm of W.S. White will be paying us a visit. They
will be visiting each department and speaking briefly with
some of you and later on one or two of them will be
spending some considerable time in each department in
turn.

I would like you to extend a warm welcome to these
gentlemen and to give them your wholehearted co-
operation. They are not 'snoopers'. They are here at the
invitation of the management and they are here to help us.
They can only do so, however, if each one of us, from
managing director to filing clerk, gives them all the co-
operation we can.

I will keep you posted on the various phases of the
work and, certainly, in due course, of any changes which we
may decide to make.

New premises   **693**

You will be pleased to learn that our management
has for some time been considering building a new factory
and offices. Search for suitable land has been going on for
several months and we have now been able to acquire a
suitable plot only three miles from here, on the south side
of town.

Drawings are now being prepared and you can be
sure that I will continue to keep you in the picture as
progress is made.

694

New premises

The attached drawing is an artist's impression of our new building, which will soon be going up in Newtown Road, between Green Street and the green fields beyond.

It is too early yet to talk about moving in, but as the new building is so close by, there is no need for any of you to worry about the impending move.

695

New premises

Work began this week on our new building and we are promised completion by the late spring, weather permitting.

696

New premises

We now have tentative moving-in dates for the new building.

The factory should be able to move in by the end of March and the offices gradually, beginning the end of April.

Department heads will keep you posted.

697

House Warming

Now that we are comfortably settled into our wonderful new building, it is time to think about an official opening and house-warming party.

There will, in fact, be two events. First, there will be a house-warming party for all company employees. This will take place in the canteen at 5.00 p.m. on Friday, September 11.

Then there will be a party for the Press and our customers and suppliers. This will take place on Wednesday, September 16, and will be a sort of all-day-long 'Open House'. People will be buzzing about all over the place and you will not be able to get much work done, but you will be relied upon to act the part!

Appendix

Forms of Address

The armed services

Officers in the armed services are addressed according to rank, with either their full given name or initials, followed by the surname. For instance: Lieutenant-General C.B. Mathews; Air Commodore W.S. Lewis, RAF; Group Officer Beryl Richards, WRAF.

If an officer is titled, the service rank is given first, e.g. Admiral Sir George Fielding, Squadron Leader the Hon. F.V. James. Sub-lieutenants, midshipmen and cadets in the Royal Navy, lieutenants and second-lieutenants in the Army, and flying officers and pilot officers in the Royal Air Force are referred to as 'Mr' and therefore their letters should be addressed 'Esq.', followed by RN, the name of their regiment, or RAF respectively for each of the services, e.g. F. Brown, Esq., RN; J.J. Jackson, Esq., Coldstream Guards; N.J. Watson, Esq., RAF. Decorations should be given after the name, e.g. Captain E.H. Dawson, DSO, RN.

It has to be admitted that these forms are more honoured in the breach than in the observance and this for two reasons: first of all the junior officers rather like to be addressed by rank and, secondly, people outside the services are seldom acquainted with the correct forms of address and tend to assume that service titles are in order.

The diplomatic service

A British Consul abroad is addressed: A.B. Richards, Esq. (or Miss, Mrs or Ms, as the case may be) HM Consul at . . . (name of city or town). A foreign ambassador to the Court of St James is addressed as follows: To His Excellency (or Her Excellency) the French (or as the case may be) Ambassador.

Civic dignitaries

Lord Mayor. The Lord Mayors of London, York, Belfast, Dublin, Cardiff, Sydney, Melbourne, Adelaide, Brisbane and Hobart alone have the privilege of being styled 'Right Hon.'. Letters to them should be addressed: To the Right Hon. The Lord Mayor of . . ., or To the Lord Mayor of . . .

The other cities which have a Lord Mayor are: Birmingham, Bradford, Bristol, Coventry, Hull, Leeds, Leicester, Liverpool, Manchester, Newcastle, Norwich, Nottingham, Plymouth, Portsmouth, Sheffield, Stoke-on-Trent. In these cases, envelopes should be addressed as follows: To the Right Worshipful The Lord Mayor of . . . (or Lady Mayoress of . . .).

In Scotland the equivalent status of a Lord Mayor is Lord Provost. The Lord Provost of Edinburgh is entitled to the words 'The Right Hon.' before his name. The Lord Provost of Glasgow is addressed as The Right Hon. The Lord Provost of Glasgow. The others are simply addressed as 'The Lord Provost of . . .'. Their wives do not share their title.

Lady Mayoress. The wife of a lord mayor (lady mayoress) is styled: To the Right Hon. The Lady . . ., but only during her husband's terms of mayoralty.

Mayor (man or woman). If of a city: To the Right Worshipful the Mayor of . . .
If of a borough: To the Worshipful the Mayor of . . .

Provost. To the Provost of . . .

Sheriff. The Sheriff of . . .

Justice of the Peace. John Brown, Esq., JP or Mrs, Miss or Ms Margaret Brown, JP.

The Legal Profession

The Lord Chancellor. To the Right Hon. the Lord High Chancellor.

Lord Chief Justice. To the Right Hon. the Lord Chief Justice of England or To the Right Hon. the Lord Blank, Lord Chief Justice of England (according to rank).

Solicitor General. To the Right Hon. Sir John Blank, Solicitor-General, QC.

Judge of the High Court. To the Hon. Mr Justice Brown or To the Hon. Mrs Justice Smith, DBE (this form is used whether the judge is married or single).

Judge of County Court and Circuit Judge. His Honour Judge Blank.

Additional forms of address may be found in the following books: *Titles and Forms of Address, A Guide to their Correct Use*, Adam and Charles Black, London; *Debrett's Correct Forms* and *Crockford's Clerical Directory*, which gives forms of address for clergymen in the Church of England.

It is as well to be aware of the fact that the experts on these matters of protocol do not agree one hundred per cent with one another, yet each expert believes that he, and he alone is right. It is therefore best to keep one reference book on one's desk and to follow it consistently.